Arthur S. Terence

P. Terenti Phormio

With Notes and Introductions Intended for the Higher Forms of Public Schools

Arthur S. Terence

P. Terenti Phormio
With Notes and Introductions Intended for the Higher Forms of Public Schools

ISBN/EAN: 9783337158996

Printed in Europe, USA, Canada, Australia, Japan

Cover: Foto ©Paul-Georg Meister /pixelio.de

More available books at **www.hansebooks.com**

Clarendon Press Series

P. TERENTI

PHORMIO

WITH NOTES AND INTRODUCTIONS

INTENDED FOR THE HIGHER FORMS OF PUBLIC SCHOOLS

BY THE

REV. A. SLOMAN, M.A.

HEAD MASTER OF BIRKENHEAD SCHOOL
FORMERLY MASTER OF THE QUEEN'S SCHOLARS OF WESTMINSTER

SECOND EDITION, REVISED

Oxford
AT THE CLARENDON PRESS
1894

PREFACE.

In the text of this edition the MSS. have been followed rather than the emendations of editors, unless there seemed to be weighty reasons to the contrary. In places, however, where A is certainly corrupt, the testimony of Donatus or other Scholiasts as to readings earlier than those in the Calliopian MSS. has been sometimes accepted, when supported by intrinsic probability. In all but a few cases the limits of space have precluded a full statement of the arguments for and against doubtful readings, but in no instance has a decision been made without careful consideration of all sides of the question.

In a School edition it has been thought better to print the letter *v*, and to adopt the modernised spelling of the MSS., except where the orthography in Terence's time was demonstrably different: e.g. *o* is substituted for *u* after another *u* or *v*; *quor, quoius, quoi*, etc., appear for *cur, cuius, cui*, etc., and *-is* for *-es* in the accusative plural of such words of the third declension as form the genitive plural in *-ium*.

As regards the spelling of verbs or adjectives compounded with prepositions no rigid uniformity has been observed, because none existed in the republican period. Assimilation took place in the commoner words, and in certain combinations of letters (e.g. *m* and *p*), much earlier than in others. Accordingly *conraditur* is read, but *comparatum* (40–1), and so on. In this respect the text follows that of Fleckeisen.

This Play, like its three predecessors in the same series, has been carefully expurgated for use in Schools.

It is hoped that the stage directions, which have been mainly suggested by practical experience at Westminster, may be of real service.

Constant use has been made of the editions of Umpfenbach, Fleckeisen, Dziatzko, Wagner, Bond and Walpole,—the first two on textual questions only,—with less frequent reference to those of Bentley, Zeune (containing the commentaries of Donatus), Stallbaum, Parry, and Davies. References are made to Roby's School Latin Grammar as more likely to be generally accessible than his larger work.

I have to thank my former fellow-worker, C. E. Freeman, Esq., of Park House School, Southborough, to whose accurate scholarship our editions of the *Trinummus* and *Andria* owed so much, for his courteous permission to make use of any matter which appeared in one of the Plays above mentioned as our joint production. I must also express my obligations to the Rev. R. F. Dale for his kindness in reading through the notes and making some valuable suggestions.

A. S.

BIRKENHEAD SCHOOL:
June, 1887.

PREFACE TO SECOND EDITION.

THE whole work has been carefully revised, and, it is hoped, improved. Among my critics I have especially to express my obligations to my friends, the late Mr. J. H. Onions of Christ Church, and Mr. St. G. Stock of Pembroke College, Oxford, several of whose suggestions have been adopted.

A. S.

BIRKENHEAD SCHOOL, 1890.

CONTENTS.

	PAGE
INTRODUCTION:	
ROMAN COMEDY AND TERENCE	9
PLOT AND CHARACTERS OF PHORMIO	19
METRES AND PROSODY OF PHORMIO	25
ACCIDENCE AND SYNTAX OF PHORMIO	31
CODICES OF TERENCE	35
TEXT OF PHORMIO (WITH STAGE DIRECTIONS)	37
LIST OF METRES OF PHORMIO	105
NOTES TO PHORMIO	107
INDEX TO NOTES	172

INTRODUCTION.

ROMAN COMEDY AND TERENCE.

First beginnings of Dramatic Representations at Rome. The natural bent of the Roman character was too serious and too prosaic to favour the growth of a national drama. More than five hundred years had elapsed since the foundation of the city, before a play of any kind was produced on the Roman stage, and even then it was but a rude adaptation of a foreign work by a foreign author.

Fescennine Verses. Yet there had long existed the germs whence a drama might, under other circumstances, have sprung. The unrestrained merriment of the harvest-home at time of vintage found expression, in Latium as in Greece, in extemporised dialogues more or less metrical in character, and much more than less coarse in expression. The lively genius of the Greeks had from such rude beginnings developed a regular Comedy as early as the sixth century B.C. But, among the Romans, although these rustic effusions were at a very early date sufficiently well established to receive a definite name, *Carmina Fescennina*, from Fescennia, a town in Etruria; yet they never rose above gross personalities and outrageous scurrility[1]. When this license was checked by a stringent clause in

---

[1] See Horace Ep. 2. 1. 145 seqq.
Fescennina per hunc inventa licentia morem
Versibus alternis opprobria rustica fudit,
Libertasque recurrentes accepta per annos
Lusit amabiliter, donec iam saevus apertam

the Laws of the Twelve Tables, the Fescennine verses became merely a generic name for improvised songs, not always very refined, at weddings, triumphs, or other festal occasions.

Saturae. According to Livy 7. 2, the first '*ludi scenici*' were introduced at Rome 361 B.C. to appease the anger of the gods who had sent a pestilence on the city.

It seems certain that about this time a stage was erected in the Circus at the *Ludi Maximi*, and the first three days of the festival were henceforth occupied with recitations, music and dancing. Performers from Etruria, called *ludiones*, danced to the music of the flute without words or descriptive action; but the strolling minstrels of Latium (*grassatores, spatiatores*) soon took advantage of the stage to recite their chants with appropriate music and gesture. These performances were named from their miscellaneous character **Saturae**[1]. They were composed in the rugged Saturnian metre, with no connected plot, and did not admit of dialogue.

Fabulae Atellanae. A nearer approach to dramatic form was made in the **Fabulae Atellanae**, broad farces with stock characters, e. g. Maccus, Pappus, Bucco, and Dossenus, analogous to the clown, pantaloon, and harlequin of an English pantomime. Each character had its traditional mask, and the pieces were originally played only by amateurs at private theatricals; but when translations from Greek dramas had monopolised the Roman stage, the Atellan farce was adopted as

---

In rabiem coepit verti iocus, et per honestas
Ire domos impune minax. Doluere cruento
Dente lacessiti, fuit intactis quoque cura
Condicione super communi, quin etiam lex
Poenaque lata, malo quae nollet carmine quemquam
Describi: vertere modum formidine fustis
Ad bene dicendum delectandumque redacti.

[1] From *lanx satura*, a dish of mixed food. The later *Saturae* or Miscellanies, with which we are familiar from the works of Horace, Juvenal, and Persius, were introduced by Lucilius, who died 103 B.C. Cf. Hor. Sat. 1. 10.

an after-piece, like the Satyric drama among the Greeks, and was regularly performed by professional actors. The name *Atellanae*, from Atella, an Oscan town near Capua, gave rise to the erroneous supposition that these farces were performed at Rome in the Oscan dialect ; whereas it was only in accordance with Roman custom to give to dramatic performances a local name which could offend no national prejudices. The records of these plays are scanty, but they appear to have presented extravagant caricatures of special classes, trades, or occurrences, and their grotesque situations and lively humour secured them a lasting place in popular favour.

Laws regulating Dramatic Performances. The failure of the Romans to produce a national drama was due, not only to their national 'gravity,' but also to the rigid censorship of the laws. Any personal lampoon, any ill-advised criticism of public affairs, met with summary chastisement. '*Fuste feritor*' was the laconic edict of the Twelve Tables : and the magistrates seem to have had plenary power to scourge any actor at any time or place that they deemed fit.

Public opinion at Rome. To legal harshness was added a moral stigma. No Roman citizen could venture to appear on a public stage without losing his character for ever. The composition and performance of plays were handed over entirely to freedmen and slaves, who did not dare to represent Roman life, or introduce Roman topics. Even the rustic raillery and amateur farces of early Rome had to lay their scene in Tuscan Fescennia or Oscan Atella.

Contact with Greek civilisation. Moreover, in addition to a national deficiency of literary instinct and ignominious legal penalties, a third cause had operated powerfully in checking any development of dramatic originality. For nearly five centuries the Romans had been engaged in a varying, yet almost ceaseless struggle for supremacy, or even for existence. The defeat of Pyrrhus, 274 B.C., and the final conquest of Tarentum and the other cities of Magna Graecia a few years later, left them undisputed masters of the whole peninsula. They were thus brought into close contact with Greek civilisation at the very moment when they had leisure to attend to it. There began at once to arise an ever-increasing demand for a better education for the Roman youth, and for more varied amusements for the Roman populace. The satisfaction of these demands was delayed by the First Punic War, 264-241 B.C.

Livius Andronicus. In 240 B.C. Livius Andronicus, a Tarentine captive who received his freedom for educating the sons of Livius Salinator, produced on the Roman stage[1] a drama translated from the Greek. He also translated the Odyssey into Saturnian verse as an educational text-book, which was still in use in the boyhood of Horace[2]. Thus at Rome the beginnings both of Epic and Dramatic poetry were due not so much to poetical inspiration as to the needs of the school-room and the Circus. As might be expected in work thus done to order, there was little artistic merit. The few fragments which remain seem crude and barbarous, and we may well believe that the books were never again opened when the rod of an Orbilius was no longer dreaded.

Old Athenian Comedy. There could be no doubt as to the school of Attic Comedy to be chosen for imitation. The Old Comedy of Eupolis, Cratinus or Aristophanes, essentially political in its subjects, abounding in topical allusions and trenchant satire of public men and public matters, could not have been reproduced on a Roman stage.

Middle Comedy. Even the poets of the Middle Comedy, who satirised classes rather than individuals or travestied schools

---

[1] *Serus enim Graecis admovit acumina chartis,
Et post Punica bella quietus quaerere coepit,
Quid Sophocles et Thespis et Aeschylus utile ferrent.*
Hor. Ep. 2. 1. 161–163.

[2] *Non equidem insector delendave carmina Livi
Esse reor, memini quae plagosum mihi parvo
Orbilium dictare.*
Hor. Ep. 1. 2. 1. 69–71.

of philosophy, would have seemed to the stern censors of the
Republic far too free, and would have been almost unintelligible
to the majority of Romans.

New Comedy. The New Comedy was alone available. This
was the name given to a school of dramatists, of whom the best
known are Philemon, Diphilus, Apollodorus of Carystus, and
above all Menander. They wrote at a period (340-260 B.C.)
when the power of Macedon had crushed the liberty of Greece.
Political life was dead; social life was idle and corrupt. The
natural products of such a period of decay were the 'Society'
plays of the New Comedy. Their aim was merely to give
amusing sketches of every-day life[1]. The savage satire of
Aristophanes only survived in good-humoured banter. The
keen strife of Conservatism against Democracy was replaced by
intrigues of amorous youths or crafty slaves to outwit the head
of the family. The interest of these plays was not local but
cosmopolitan. Human nature is pretty much the same in all
ages, and so these plays were naturally suited for the Roman
stage. They were amusing, without the slightest tendency to
criticise points of national interest, or otherwise offend against
the strict regulations of the Roman magistrates.

Cn. Naevius, who flourished 235-204 B.C., the first imitator
of Livius Andronicus, a Campanian of great ability and force of
character, did indeed dare to write with something of Aristo-
phanic freedom. But his temerity in assailing the haughty
Metelli, and even the mighty Africanus himself, led first to im-
prisonment and afterwards to banishment. The experiment
was not repeated.

Plautus and Terence. Between 230 and 160 B.C. the writers
of Comedy were fairly numerous[2], but only two have bequeathed

---

[1] Cf. Cic. Rep. 4. 11 *imitationem vitae, speculum consuetudinis, im-
aginem veritatis.*

[2] e.g. Caecilius, Licinius, Atilius, and others. Ennius, whose fame
rests on his Epic poem, also adapted Greek plays, chiefly tragedies, to
the Roman stage.

to posterity more than scattered fragments. These two are Titus Maccius Plautus and Publius Terentius Afer.

Life and Works of Terence. Plautus died in 184 B.C. Terence was born in 195 B.C. at Carthage, whence his cognomen 'Afer.' He was a slave, but must early have shown signs of ability, for his master, Terentius Lucanus, gave him a good education, and before long his freedom. His talents gained him admission to the literary clique, known as the Scipionic circle, the fashionable representatives of the new Hellenic culture. Scipio Aemilianus was the centre of the coterie, which included Laelius, L. Furius Philus, Sulpicius Gallus, Q. Fabius Labeo, M. Popillius, the philosopher Panaetius, and the historian Polybius. These being men of education and taste, unreservedly recognised the immeasurable superiority of Greek literature as compared with the rude efforts of their native writers. To present to a Roman audience a faithful reproduction of the best Hellenic models, in pure and polished Latin, seemed to them the ideal of literary excellence. Style was more valued than strength, correctness of form more than originality of thought. Such was the literary atmosphere which Terence breathed; and his enemies, not confining themselves to gross aspersions on his moral character, openly affirmed that the plays produced under his name were really the work of his distinguished patrons. How far Scipio or Laelius may have had some hand in his plays can never be known; Terence at any rate did not care to refute the report which doubtless flattered his noble friends, but rather prided himself on the intimacy and approbation of so select a circle[1]. All the plays of Terence, as

---

[1] *Nam quod isti dicunt malevoli, homines nobilis
Eum adiutare adsidueque una scribere;
Quod illi maledictum vehemens esse existumant,
Eam laudem hic ducit maximam, quom illis placet,
Qui vobis univorsis et populo placent,
Quorum opera in bello, in otio, in negotio
Suo quisque tempore usus 'st sine superbia.*
                              Adelphi Prol. 15-21.

of Plautus, were *Comoediae palliatae*, i.e. plays wherein the scene and characters are Greek, as opposed to *Comoediae togatae*, where the scene is laid in Rome or at least in Italy. National tragedies and dramas were called *Fabulae Praetextae*.

Terence's first comedy, the Andria, was produced 166 B.C. Suetonius relates that when this play was offered to the Aediles, the young author was told to submit it to the judgment of Caecilius. Terence arrived when the veteran poet was at supper, and being in mean attire was seated on a stool near the table. But he had read no more than a few lines, when Caecilius bade him take a place upon his couch, and bestowed high commendation on the play. As Caecilius died in 168 B.C., the Andria must have been in manuscript at least two years before its performance, and some colour is given to the above anecdote by the mention which Terence makes in the Prologue of the ill-natured criticisms of Luscius Lanuvinus. The Hecyra, his second play, proved his least successful one. At its first performance in 165 B.C., the audience deserted the theatre to look at some boxers; a similar fate attended a second representation in 160 B.C., and only the personal intercession of the manager, Ambivius Turpio, secured it a hearing at all. The Heauton Timorumenos appeared in 163, the Eunuchus and Phormio in 161, the Adelphi in 160. In the same year Terence visited Greece, either to study for himself Athenian manners and customs, or, as some assert, to escape the persecution of his enemies. According to one account[1] he perished by shipwreck in 159 B.C., as he was returning to Italy with no less than 108 of Menander's comedies translated into Latin. A more general belief was that he died at Stymphalus, in Arcadia, from grief on hearing of the loss of his MSS., which he had sent on before him by sea. Porcius Licinus narrates that his noble patrons suffered him to die in such abject poverty that he had not even a lodging at Rome whither a slave might have brought news of his death. This is probably untrue, for Suetonius writes that he

---

[1] Cf. Suetonius, Vita Terenti 4-5.

left gardens of twenty jugera in extent on the Appian Way, and his daughter afterwards married a Roman knight.

In personal appearance Terence is said to have been of middle height, with a slight figure and reddish-brown hair. Of his character we know nothing, save what can be gathered from his prologues. These indicate a lack of independence and confidence. He evidently feels that he is not a popular poet. He never professes to be more than an adapter from Greek models; imitation, not creation, was the object of his art.

Contrast of Plautus and Terence. The sensitive *protégé* of patrician patrons has none of the vigorous personality of Plautus. Indeed, though the literary activity of the two poets is only separated by a single generation, their works belong to different epochs of literature. Plautus wrote for the people, he aimed at the broad effect on the stage, his fun was natural and not unfrequently boisterous. Circumstances forced him to adapt foreign plays and lay his scenes in foreign cities, but he was not careful to disguise his true nationality, and freely introduced Roman names, allusions, and customs wherever they might contribute to the dramatic effect on the heterogeneous audience which crowded to the gratuitous entertainments of a Roman holiday.

Between such plays and the polished productions of Terence there is a world of difference. Terence sought the approbation, not of the uncultured masses, but of a select circle of literary men. His highest aim was to produce in the purest Latin a perfect representation of the comedies of Menander and his school. His cardinal virtues, as a writer, were correctness of language and consistency of character. His scene is always laid at Athens, and very rarely in his six plays can be found an allusion which is distinctively Roman. Indeed, the whole tone of his writings was cosmopolitan. Human nature, under the somewhat common-place conditions of every-day life in a civilised community, was his subject; *Homo sum, humani nihil a me alienum puto,* was his motto. His plays breathe a spirit of broad-minded liberality, and their simple unaffected style, the

ROMAN COMEDY AND TERENCE. 17

easy yet pointed dialogue, the terse and dramatic descriptions, and the admirable delicacy of the portrayal of character, won from the cultured taste of the Augustan age a more favourable verdict[1] than could have been expected from the rude and unlettered masses who most enjoyed the broad fun of a boisterous farce. The above characteristics secured for Terence considerable attention at the Renaissance in Europe. In England several of the minor dramatists are under obligations to him; while in France his influence profoundly affected Molière, and is in no small degree responsible for the long-continued servitude of the French drama to the 'unities' of time and place which have so cramped its free development.

As might be expected, the characters in Terence, though admirably drawn, are rather commonplace. No personality in his plays stands out in the memory like that of Tyndarus in the *Captivi*, or Stasimus in the *Trinummus*. Two old men, one irascible and the other mild, both usually the dupes of their sons and an intriguing slave; two young men, one of strong character and the other weak, both amorous and somewhat unscrupulous as to the means of gratifying their passion; a dignified and elderly gentleman; an anxious mother; a devoted servant; a rascally slave dealer: these form the stock characters of Terentian comedy and recur with somewhat wearisome monotony. Nor does the standard of morality rise above a conventional

---

[1] Afranius writes:
    Terentio non similem dices quempiam.
Cicero writes:
    Tu quoque, qui solus lecto sermone, Terenti,
    Conversum expressumque Latina voce Menandrum
    In medium nobis sedatis vocibus effers,
    Quidquid come loquens atque omnia dulcia dicens.
Horace, Ep. 2. 1. 59, records the general verdict:
    dicitur ...
    Vincere Caecilius gravitate, Terentius arte.
Volcatius, on the other hand, places Terence below Naevius, Plautus, Caecilius, Licinius, and Atilius.

respectability and a civilised consideration for others, except where the natural impulses inspire a generous disposition with something of nobility.

The discerning criticism of Caesar nearly expresses the more matured judgment of modern times:

> *Tu quoque, tu in summis, O dimidiate Menander,*
> *Poneris et merito, puri sermonis amator.*
> *Lenibus atque utinam scriptis adiuncta foret vis*
> *Comica, ut aequato virtus polleret honore*
> *Cum Graecis neque in hac despectus parte iaceres;*
> *Unum hoc maceror ac doleo tibi deesse, Terenti.*

Not that Terence was devoid of humour; but his humour is so delicate and refined that it must often have fallen flat upon the stage. When his plays are well known their subtle satire and polished wit can be appreciated; but there is without doubt an absence of energy and action (Caesar's *vis comica*), which prevented his pieces from being dramatically successful. An audience must be educated up to his plays before it can perceive their many excellences.

THE EXTANT COMEDIES OF TERENCE.

ANDRIA, produced at Ludi Megalenses . . 166 B.C.
HECYRA, failed to obtain a hearing at Ludi
    Megalenses . . . . 165 B.C.
HEAUTON TIMORUMENOS, produced at Ludi
    Megalenses . . . . 163 B.C.
EUNUCHUS, produced at Ludi Megalenses . 161 B.C.
PHORMIO, produced at Ludi Romani . . . 161 B.C.
ADELPHI, produced at Ludi Funerales of
    Aemilius Paullus . . . . 160 B.C.

The Hecyra was put on the stage a second time, but again failed, at the Ludi Funerales of Aemilius Paullus in 160 B.C.; and finally was played at the Ludi Romani in the same year.

THE PLOT AND CHARACTERS OF THE PHORMIO.

The scene of this play is, as usual, laid at Athens. The characters of the two old men, so familiar to readers of Terentian comedy, are represented by the brothers Demipho and Chremes, Athenian citizens of good position and some fortune. The former has a son named Antipho; the latter is husband to Nausistrata, of whom he stands in considerable awe, and father of Phaedria. Nausistrata has inherited from her father property in the island of Lemnos, whither Chremes goes year by year to collect the rents and realise the produce of the farms. While on one of these visits he clandestinely marries, under the feigned name of Stilpho, a Lemnian lady, and has by her a daughter named Phanium, born sixteen years before the opening scene of the play. This family is supported out of the income derived from the property of Nausistrata, who imagines that it is only one example of Chremes' general incapacity that he brings home so much less money than the estate formerly yielded.

Demipho is aware of this unlawful connexion, and has moreover agreed to marry his son Antipho to Phanium, passing her off as a distant relation of the family.

The play opens at a time when Demipho and Chremes are both absent from Athens, the former in Cilicia on a visit to an old friend who promised him a most profitable investment, the latter on a journey to Lemnos, whence he intends to bring Phanium for the projected marriage with Antipho. Upon his arrival, however, he finds that both mother and daughter have left the island in search of him. They arrive safely, but being unable to discover any one in Athens named Stilpho, are reduced to great poverty and distress. Overcome by her anxieties the mother falls ill and dies, leaving Phanium in charge of a trusty old nurse, Sophrona.

During this period the two young men Antipho and Phaedria

are left at Athens in charge of Demipho's confidential slave Geta.

Act I. In the opening scenes Geta narrates his experiences to his friend Davus. Finding it impossible to control a pair of wild youths, he gives up the attempt, and lets them follow their own devices.

Phaedria first falls violently in love with a music-girl named Pamphila, who is in the hands of a slave-dealer, Dorio, on sale for thirty minae (£120). As Phaedria has no money, he can do nothing but escort his lady-love to and from the school where she is completing her education.

Just at this time Antipho is told a touching story of a beauty in distress at a funeral. He goes to see, and it proves to be none other than Phanium weeping over her mother's corpse.

The young man is at once captivated by her charms, but dares not marry a penniless girl in his father's absence. In his perplexity he lays the case before Phormio, a shrewd parasite, from whom the play is named. Phormio takes up the matter with zest. He has often been entertained at Antipho's house, and has moreover a natural turn for intrigue. Pretending to be a kinsman of Phanium, he trumps up a fictitious story that Antipho is her nearest relation and so by Athenian law under obligation to marry her. Antipho is summoned before the courts, of course makes no attempt to rebut Phormio's evidence, and so is bound over to marry Phanium, which he does forthwith. His happiness is, however, soon clouded by the dread of his father's wrath, and he pours forth his troubles (Sc. 3) into the unsympathetic ears of his cousin, who considers that he himself is alone deserving of pity. Geta now (Sc. 4) brings the news of Demipho's arrival. Antipho cannot be induced to face his father, and runs away, leaving Phaedria and Geta to fight his battles for him.

Both do their best to calm down the irascible old gentleman, who comes on (Sc. 5) fuming at the news of his son's unauthorised marriage. In spite of all that can be said, Act I closes with his determination to seek legal advice and fight the matter out with Phormio.

Act II introduces us to Phormio, who confidently assures Geta that he will make everything all right, and gives a lively picture of a parasite's easy life. The conversation is interrupted by the appearance of Demipho (Sc. 2) with three advisers. Phormio at once assumes a high hand. He defies Demipho to interfere with a judgment formally given in a court of law, and threatens to sue him for heavy damages if he ventures to turn Phanium, as he threatens, out of doors. Demipho is furious, but cannot outface the parasite. Each of his three friends gives a different opinion, and he is left in a state of greater perplexity than before. Finally he decides to await his brother's return, and goes off to make enquiries at the Peiraeus.

Thereupon Antipho reappears (Sc. 4) and learns from Geta what has occurred. They are quickly joined by Phaedria and Dorio. The slave-dealer has had an offer for the music-girl, and with cynical brutality repudiates his engagement to give Phaedria some time longer to procure the necessary money. The young lover is in the depths of despair, but is somewhat cheered by Geta's promise to raise the thirty minae by hook or by crook.

Act III. In the interval between Acts II and III Chremes has returned. Demipho is explaining to him the position of affairs when Geta appears, prepared to carry out a scheme concocted between himself and Phormio to obtain from the old men the money required by Phaedria. He tells the two fathers that zealous for their interests he has sounded Phormio as to what he would take to get Phanium safely out of the way by marrying her himself. Phormio alleges that he is engaged to another girl, but, as a great favour to Demipho, will throw over his *fiancée* on payment of the sum of thirty minae as dowry for Phanium.

Demipho is furious at this extravagant demand; but Chremes, anxious to get his Lemnian daughter married to Antipho and so avoid the awkward questions which might be asked by a stranger, agrees to provide the money from his wife's income. All this has been overheard by Antipho in the background. He is nearly beside himself with anger at what he supposes to be Geta's treachery, and grief at the prospect of being compelled to divorce his young wife. He is only very partially reassured by Geta's explanations, and goes off to tell Phaedria of the scheme and its success as Demipho and Chremes reappear with the money. Geta conducts Demipho to settle matters with Phormio. Chremes, left alone, is considering how he can find out his wife and daughter from Lemnos, when, to his utter amazement, Sophrona, their faithful servant, comes out of Demipho's house. His bewilderment is intensified on hearing that the mother is dead and the daughter married to Antipho. At first he thinks that, in unconscious imitation of his uncle, the young man has married two wives, but when at length he realises that Phormio's ward is one and the same as his own daughter, his joy and thankfulness know no bounds, and he at once goes into his brother's house to see the bride.

In **Act IV** we find Demipho returning with Geta from his business with Phormio. He fetches Nausistrata from her house, as Chremes had requested that she should be asked to break the news to Phanium with reference to her projected match with Phormio. But as they approach the door out comes Chremes full of excitement at the unlooked-for turn which events have taken. An amusing scene follows. Chremes tries to stop Demipho from taking further action, but cannot give any intelligible reason in Nausistrata's presence. He finally manages to get his wife dismissed, and takes Demipho into the house to communicate his great piece of news. As soon as they have disappeared Antipho enters, quickly followed by Phormio, in high spirits at having secured the money for Phaedria who has lost no time in having his Pamphila formally set at liberty. Geta bursts out of the house upon them, beside himself with excitement. By an adroit piece of eavesdropping he has learnt the secret about Phanium, the importance

PHORMIO: PLOT AND CHARACTERS. 23

of which is fully grasped by Phormio, who retires to prepare for the next stage of his intrigue.

Act V opens with a stormy scene between Phormio and the two old gentlemen. The parasite demands Phanium as his bride in accordance with the compact. Demipho says that he has changed his mind and insists that the thirty minae should be refunded. Phormio indignantly refuses, and roundly reviles them both for their childish indecision. Demipho, losing all patience, tries to hurry Phormio off to the law-courts, whereupon the parasite plays his trump card. He openly proclaims his knowledge of Chremes' Lemnian family, and threatens to tell all to Nausistrata. This brings matters to a climax. Demipho and Chremes endeavour to drag Phormio away from the house and a violent struggle ensues, which is ended by the appearance of Nausistrata, summoned by the parasite's stentorian lungs. Chremes, to his utter confusion, has to hear the story of his misdeeds poured into the ears of his injured wife. Nausistrata is wildly indignant, Phormio insolently triumphant. He invites the public to Chremes' 'funeral obsequies,' and further tells of Phaedria's marriage and of the trick by which the purchase money was secured. At this news Chremes begins to fume, but is at once set down with the crushing retort from his imperious spouse that his son might well have one wife, if the father had two. Demipho's mediation at last effects a provisional reconciliation. As a reward for his services, and as a punishment to Chremes, Phormio obtains from Nausistrata an invitation to dinner, of which he will no doubt constantly avail himself, and they all go into the house as the curtain falls.

The story of the Play will have already indicated the main outlines of the several characters. In naming the Play after Phormio, Terence showed a just appreciation of the importance of the part. The individuality of the parasite is strongly marked. Shrewd and unscrupulous as to means, avowedly a 'bird of prey' who lives on the weakness or the vice of his neighbours, he yet displays an active sympathy and *bon-homie* in his dealings with the young men, which redeem his rascality from utter baseness. He may be a rogue, but he is no hypocrite, like Chremes.

Antipho and Phaedria are rather common-place, and, unlike Aeschinus and Ctesipho in the Adelphi, are very similar in character. Both are frank and affectionate, but entirely wanting in mental ballast or moral principle, the slaves of their passions and mere puppets in the hands of Phormio, or even of the servant Geta.

On the other hand, the personality of the two old gentlemen is sharply drawn and skilfully worked out. Demipho is an irascible miser, with a domineering disposition which ill brooks contradiction, and a love of money which made him ready to expose his brother to public shame rather than submit to the loss of thirty minae.

Chremes is a life-like portrait of a weak and hen-pecked husband. He has no more principle than his son with much less honesty, and richly deserves the unenviable position in which we leave him.

Nausistrata is a strong-minded shrew, who despised and persecuted her feeble husband, but she seems to have been liberal enough in advancing a large sum to Demipho, nor does she grudge it to Phaedria when she learns the truth. The violence of her temper affords the only extenuation for the infidelity of Chremes, and brings dramatic retribution on her own head.

Of the other characters little need be said. Dorio enjoys the unenviable reputation of being the most repulsive and rascally slave-dealer in Roman Comedy: Geta is faithlessly faithful in helping the young men to cheat his master: Sophrona has the usual characteristic of old nurses depicted by Terence, devoted attachment to her mistress: the 'advocates' are concisely, though unintentionally, humorous.

Artistically considered the Phormio occupies a middle place among the comedies of Terence. In it we find nothing so farcical as the 'baby-scene' in the Andria, nor has it the exquisite polish and pervading moral purpose of the Adelphi. But the dialogue is more pointed and the interest better sustained than in the earlier play, while what is lost in finish is gained in vigour when compared with the later. Molière has made the Phormio the basis of a farce, *Les Fourberies de Scapin*, but no impartial critic would prefer the copy to the original.

METRES AND PROSODY.

The object of this Introduction is to explain briefly the metres employed by Terence in the Phormio, and to clear up such apparent difficulties of Prosody as may remain after the general scheme of the metres is understood.

These metres are Iambic and Trochaic, which receive their names from being composed of iambi or trochees, as the case may be, or of some other feet, considered to be equivalent: and the lines are further subdivided according to the number of metres which they contain, and according to their complete or incomplete form. In iambic and trochaic lines a series of two feet is called a *metre* (or *dipodia*), and the name of the line corresponds to the number of these metres; thus an iambic trimeter is an iambic line containing three metres or six feet; a trochaic tetrameter is a trochaic line containing four metres or eight feet. Again, some lines have a number of complete feet; these are called acatalectic; while others are called catalectic, because the last foot is incomplete. Thus a trochaic tetrameter catalectic is a trochaic line of four metres or eight feet, wanting the last syllable, and really containing only seven feet and a half.

I. IAMBIC.

(*a*) **Iambic Trimeter Acatalectic, or Senarius**: (620[1]); all the plays of Terence begin with it.

---

[1] These figures, here and below, indicate the number of lines of the metre in question in this Play.

(*b*) **Iambic Tetrameter Acatalectic**, called **Octonarius** from its eight complete feet. (116.)

(*c*) **Iambic Tetrameter Catalectic**, called **Septenarius** from its seven complete feet. (57.)

(*d*) **Iambic Dimeter Acatalectic, or Quaternarius.** (3.)

These lines consist in their pure form of iambi; but the spondee, tribrach, anapaest, and dactyl are admitted in all feet except the last, which must be an iambus, unless, of course, the verse is catalectic. Moreover, as the Tetrameter is *Asynartete*, i.e. regarded as being composed of two verses, with the division after the fourth foot, that foot is usually an iambus; and such words as *ego*, *tibi*, *cedo*, are allowed to stand there as if at the end of a senarius. In any iambic metre an anapaest is occasionally resolved into a Proceleusmatic ($\smile\smile\smile\smile$), which is most commonly in the first foot, and composed of two distinct pairs of syllables. Cf. 48, 133, 276, 370, 394, 707, 733, 762, 768, 776, 795, 966, 968, 983, 999.

II. Trochaic.

(*a*) **Trochaic Tetrameter Acatalectic, or Octonarius.** (19.)

(*b*) **Trochaic Tetrameter Catalectic, or Septenarius.** (237.)

(*c*) **Trochaic Dimeter Catalectic.** (2.)

These lines consist in their pure form of trochees; the spondee, tribrach, anapaest, and dactyl are also admitted. But only the trochee, tribrach, and sometimes dactyl are found in the seventh foot of the Septenarius. In Trochaic Septenarii the last syllable is always considered as long: cf. 318, 319, 321. Trochaic, like Iambic Tetrameters, are considered to be divided after the fourth foot, but in neither metre is this division constantly observed. As the Trochaic metre is more quick and lively than the Iambic, it is naturally employed in scenes where strong feeling and excitement are represented.

Besides the above, 485 is an irregular line, apparently consisting of one trochee with a syllable over.

PROSODY.

The rules of prosody, as commonly taught, must be considerably modified, if we are to understand the scansion of Plautus and Terence. It must always be remembered that the poets of the late days of the Republic and their successors were writing in a literary dialect, not in the language of everyday life. The quantity of any syllable was regarded as rigidly fixed, just as we might find it marked in a dictionary. But in reading the comic poets we find that *accent* must be considered as well as quantity. Scansion was determined by the ear, not by any hard and fast rules. Just as in Shakesperian verse *loved* may be scanned as of one syllable or of two, and the same word may be pronounced as long or short according to its position, so in Terence *eius, huius, quoius,* etc., may be monosyllabic or dissyllabic, and the same syllable may be used with a different quantity according to the requirements of the metre. This latter variation of quantity is however not arbitrary, but conforms to a general law, which may be thus stated.

When the metrical accent[1] **falls on the first syllable of an Iambus, or on the syllable before or after an Iambus, the second syllable of the Iambus may be shortened.**

Accordingly in Iambic metre,

(a) $-\acute{\smile}-=-\acute{\smile}\smile$, (b) $\smile-\acute{-}=\smile\smile\acute{-}$:

in Trochaic metre,

(c) $\acute{-}\smile-=\acute{-}\smile\smile$,

(d) $\acute{\smile}--=\acute{\smile}\smile-$, (e) $\acute{\smile}-\smile=\acute{\smile}\smile\smile$.

It will be noted that in the following examples some of the shortened syllables would by the ordinary rules be long by nature, others long by position; and that the 'Iambic Law' applies equally to a combination made up of more than one word.

---

[1] In Iambic metre the accent falls on the second syllable of all feet except anapaests and proceleusmatics, which are accented on the third: in Trochaic metre the accent is always on the first syllable.

(a) 10 *actóris opera mágĭs stetísse.*
  787 *factŭm volo: ăc pol mĭnŭs queo virĭ́ cúlpa, quăm me dígnum est.* (Here *virĭ́* illustrates *b*.)
  922 *argĕ́ntum rúrsum iŭbĕ́ rescríbi, Phŏ́rmio.*
Other examples are 800 *cŏ́rdi quid ĭstuc,* 972 *quin nŏvŏ́.*

(b) 143 *vel ŏccídito.*
  261 *darĭ́ mi in conspĕ́ctum.*
  266 *hic ĭn nóxia est, ĭ́lle ăd dĕ́fendĕ́ndam caŭsam adĕ́st.*
  434 *senĕctútem oblĕ́ctet.*
  439 *dicăm tibi ĭnpĭngam grăndem.*
  806 *neque ĭntĕ́llegĕ́s.*
  902 *verĕbámini.*
The following are in Proceleusmatics:
  370 *ob hănc ĭnĭmicítias.*
  707 *angŭis per ĭnplŭ́vium dĕ́cidit.*

This form of shortening, i.e. where the accent falls on the syllable after the iambus, is by far the most frequent, and is very common in the first foot. Examples are too numerous to quote at length.

(c) 529 *nam hĭc me huiŭ́s modĭ́ scibat ĕ́sse.*
  546 *sĕd parŭmne ĕ́st quod.*
  557 *quăntum opus ĕ́st tibi ărgĕ́nti.*
  739 *cŏ́nloquăr. quis hĭc lŏ́quitur.*

(d) 209 *quĭ́d hĭc contĕ́rimus ŏ́peram.*
  516 *ĭ́dem hic tĭbi quod bonĭ́ promĕ́ritus.*
  564 *scio ĕ́sse exănimatăm metu.*
Other examples are 737 *mágĭs cognósco,* 852 *sĕ́d ĭ́sne est.*

(e) 342 *priŏr bibás, priór decŭmbas.*
  346 *sĕnĕx adĕ́st: vidĕ quid agas.* (Here *vidĕ* illustrates *c*.)
  563 *nŭmquid ĕ́st quŏ́d operá mea vóbis ŏ́pŭs sit. Nil, verum ăbĭ́ domum.* (Here *ĕ́st* illustrates *c*, and *opŭs* illustrates *d*.)

The so-called 'Iambic Law' may be thus accounted for. Latin pronunciation threw the accent on the penultimate of dissyllables. In the case of longer words the accent fell on the penultimate, if that syllable were long, on the antepenultimate, if the penultimate were short: e.g. sénex, regébat, réxerit. Special stress on one syllable tends to diminish the length of its neighbours. Accordingly there was a natural tendency to shorten the final syllable of an Iambus, and to obscure or drop final consonants: and this tendency was greatly strengthened when the metrical *ictus* coincided with the word-accent. When however the two did not coincide the verse-accent prevailed over the word-accent. This is most frequently exemplified in anapaestic feet of an Iambic line, when the metrical *ictus* on the third syllable of a bacchius ∪ − ⊥ changes it to an anapaest ∪ ∪ ⊥.

Conversely the *ictus* sometimes makes long a syllable which would otherwise have been short.

The final consonants most frequently disregarded are [1] *m*,— hence its elision even in Augustan poetry before a vowel or *h*,— which is often omitted in inscriptions: [2]*s*, as constantly in Lucretius and the older poets, especially when *u* precedes; and to a lesser extent *d, l, n, r, t*. Terence often avails himself of this licence, e.g. 660 *incertŭs sum* at the end of a senarius.

Similarly *opus est, factus est*, etc., may always be scanned *opu'st, factu'st* when convenient, e.g. 715, 833, etc. So also *amatus es* may metrically be *amatu's*. It was doubtless too in accordance with ordinary pronunciation that Terence some-

---

[1] Quint. 9. 4. 40, *m parum exprimitur*. Priscian 1. 38, *m obscurum in extremitate dictionum sonat.* So in Terence *enĭ(m) vero, quidĕ(m)*, etc., and probably *n* might be dropped in *ĭ(n de, i n)pluvium*, cf. 707, etc. Compare also *dedere* for *dederunt*.

[2] Cic. Or. 161. *Quod iam subrusticum videtur, olim autem politius, eorum verborum, quorum eaedem erant postremae duae litterae quae sunt in 'optumus,' postremam litteram detrahebant, nisi vocalis insequebatur. Ita non erat ea offensio in versibus quam nunc fugiunt poetae novi. Ita enim loquebamur* 'qui est omnibu' princeps,' *non* 'omnibus princeps,' *et* 'vita illa dignu' locoque,' *non* 'dignus.'

times scans *nempe* as *nĕpĕ*, e. g. 307 *nĕmpe Phórmiónem*. Note also that *mihi* and *nihil* are usually considered as monosyllabic, whether they are written as *mi* and *nil* or not: but cf. 176, 940. It seems probable that *visum est, noxia est*, etc., were pronounced *visum'st, noxia'st*, and the accents have been placed accordingly.

Besides the 'Iambic Law' and the points above mentioned, there are other causes of difference between Terentian and Augustan prosody.

I. **Indifference to double consonants,** which Terence probably did not write. Thus *ille* is often used as a pyrrhic (⌣⌣), and less frequently *ĕsse, ĕccum, quĭppe, ĭmmo*, etc.; possibly also such cases as *supĕllectile* 666, *ŏccidito* 143, etc., may be thus accounted for. Cf. Lucr. 6. 1135 *cŏruptum = corruptum*.

II. **Retention of the quantity of final syllables originally long.** This is very rare in Terence. Of the nineteen instances quoted by Wagner in his Terence, Introd., p. 14, only two are certain, viz. Phor. 9 *stetīt*, Ad. 25 *augeāt*. These instances confirm the opinion that *-it* of perf. ind. and *-at* of pres. subj. were originally long, while there is more doubt with reference to the same terminations in other tenses. In 315 *dīs* is doubtful. In the older poets, Ennius and Plautus (cf. Ritschl, Prol. 175), such long syllables are common, especially *-or* (-ωρ) in nouns, adjectives, or verbs, *-at, -et, -it* in third pers. sing. of verbs.

Lucretius seldom permits himself this licence. Mr. Munro admits only two instances of *-ēt* (though this termination is always long in Ennius), while *-āt* and *-īt* never appear except as contracted forms for *-avit, -iit*. Vergil freely lengthens *-or, -er, -ur, us, -at* (imperf.), *-et, -it*, but only in *arsis*, and usually when a pause follows the word. Note, however, that Vergil does not confine himself to syllables originally long, but admits such quantities as *supēr, puēr, capūt, procūl*, and frequently *-quē* in imitation of the Homeric τε before double consonants. Ovid regularly lengthens *periīt, subiīt, rediīt*, etc. Horace lengthens syllables in *arsis* about ten times.

III. **Synizesis** or **Synaeresis**. Almost any two vowels not separated by a consonant may be contracted into a single syllable. This is most common in the case of pronouns and *deus*, e. g. *ēum, tuōm, mēōrum, huīus, cuīus, dēos;* but we also find *rēicere* 18, *nescīo* 193, *diūtius* 182, *duās* 754, *dehortatus dortatus* 910, *quōad* 148, etc. Sometimes a word made monosyllabic by synizesis is then elided, e. g. *meum* 232. In Terence *dehinc* and *proin* are always of one syllable, *antehac* of two. On the contrary, *nunc iam* is always scanned as *nūnciām*, and is printed accordingly (*diaeresis*). Augustan poets employ Synizesis sparingly, chiefly in making consonantal *i* or *u*, as *abiete, ariete* = *abjete, arjete; tenuia* = *tenvia*, and in cases of nouns or adjectives ending in *-eus*, e.g. *aurēa*.

IV. **Hiatus** is admitted,
 (1) when there is a change of speaker, e. g. 146, 542, 963;
 (2) when the line is broken by a strong pause, e. g. Ad. 574;
 (3) after an interjection, e. g. 411, 753, 803.

Note that *O* seems to form one syllable with the following vowel by a kind of *Synaeresis* in 259, 360, 853. Occasionally a long final vowel, or a vowel before *m*, is shortened and not elided in the case of a monosyllable, e. g. *quī agět* 27, *ně agas* 419, *tě idem* 426 probably, *quăm ego* 808, *sī habet* 1041. Cf. 383, 501, 883, 911, 954, 982, 1005. Lucretius has eleven instances of this (see Munro's note on 2. 404), Vergil six, e.g. Ecl. 8. 108 *an quī amant*. Cf. Madv., 502 b.

ACCIDENCE AND SYNTAX OF THE PHORMIO.

The following is a brief synopsis of the leading peculiarities in the Accidence and Syntax of Terence, as exemplified in this Play. The references are to the notes, where the various points are treated in detail.

ACCIDENCE.

1. **Declension.**
   Genitive in *-i* for *-us* of fourth declension, 154.
   Dative in *-ae* for *-i* from *alter*, 928.
   Nominative *ipsus = ipse*, 178.
   -ce appended to cases of *hic, iste*, etc., 58, 290, 442.
   compluria = complura, 611.
   Chremes, double declension of, 63.
   preci, Dat., 547.
   Superlatives of adjectives end in *-umus*, 125.
   mirificissumum = mirificentissimum, 871.

2. **Conjugation.**
   (α) Archaic forms, *siem = sim*, and compounds of the same, as *adsient* 313, *possiet* 773; *duim = dem*, and its compounds, as *perduint*, 123.
   creduas = credas, 993, is doubtful.
   Present Infinitive Passive in *-ier*, commonly used at the end of lines, 92.
   face = fac, 309.
   faxo, etc., 308.
   (β) *-ibam = -iebam* in Imperfect Indicative, 480.
   (γ) *-ibit = -iet* in Future Simple, 765.
   (δ) *-undus*, etc. *= endus*, etc., in Gerundives and Gerunds, 22.

3. **Syncopated forms**, free use of, 13, 198.
   sis, sodes = si vis, si audes, 59, 103.
   ain, satin, etc., *= aisne, satisne*, etc., 970.

SYNTAX.

(1) **Use of Tenses.**
   (α) Present Indicative expressing '*intention*,' 486.
   (β) Present Infinitive = Future Infinitive, 532.
   (γ) Imperfect Indicative, colloquial use of, 858.

ACCIDENCE AND SYNTAX. 33

(δ) Future Perfect expressing quickness and certainty, 516.
(ε) Future Imperative = Present Imperative, 143.

(2) **Use of Moods.**
(α) Indicative in dependent sentences, 358.
(β) Indicative after *quom*, causal or concessive, 23.
(γ) Indicative for Deliberative Subjunctive, 447.
(δ) Future Indicative after *faxo*, 308.
(ε) Subjunctive in repeated questions, 122.

(3) **Verbal constructions.**
opus, personal and other constructions of, 440, 563.
impersonal use of *potest, potis est, pote*, 303, 379; *dolet*, 162.
Verbal Substantives governing cases, 293.

(4) **Use of cases.**
Accusative of Limitation and Respect, very free use of, 155, 480.
Accusative after *fungor* 281, *potior* 469, *abutor* 281, *inpendere* 180, *mederi* (perhaps) 822, *condonare* 947.
Genitive after Participles, 623.

(5) **Use of Particles.**
non or *ne* = *nonne*, 119.
ut ne = *ne* or *ut non*, 168
nil or *nullus* = *non*, 142.
qui, Ablative, free use of, 123.
Intensive Particles[1], free use of, *adeo* 389, *autem* 502-3, *enim* and *nam* 113, *ergo* 685, *etiam* 474, 542.

(6) **Ellipse**, free use of,
(α) of principal verb, 38;
(β) of Infinitive clause, 113;
(γ) of subject of Infinitive, 233.

---

[1] In the use of Intensive Particles Vergil's style presents marked similarities with that of Terence.

Besides these differences in Accidence and Syntax the plays of Terence abound, as is natural, with words or phrases used in a colloquial sense, cf. 47, 54, 79, 82, 133, 145, etc., among which may be specially mentioned proverbial sayings, cf. 78, 186, 203, 318, 419, 506, 686, 768, 780.

Tautologous and pleonastic phrases are also a characteristic of comic diction, cf. 80, 89, 164, etc.

Greek words, though not nearly so frequent as in Plautus, occur oftener than in Augustan writers, e.g. *dīcam* 127, *asymbolum* 339, *eu* 398, *gynaeceum* 862, *logi* 493, *paedagogus* 144, *palaestra* 484, *parasitus* 28.

It should however be borne in mind that most of the above points are characteristic not so much of Terence individually as of the conversational language in vogue at that period; and when writers of the Ciceronian or Augustan age descend from the artificial style then affected in literary composition—as for example Cicero in his Letters—many of these so-called peculiarities reappear.

CODICES OF TERENCE.

The MSS. of Terence fall into two classes. Class I is before the recension of Calliopius, Class II after it. Class II consists of two groups, as bracketed below.

CLASS I.

Letter of Reference.	Name of Codex.	Place where it is now kept.	Century.	Remarks.
A.	BEMBINUS.	Vatican.	IV or V.	On parchment in Rustic Capitals.

CLASS II.

Letter of Reference.	Name of Codex.	Place where it is now kept.	Century.	Remarks.
P.	PARISINUS.	Paris.	IX or X.	On parchment in minuscules.
C.	VATICANUS.	Vatican.	IX or X.	Copied by a German from the same original as P.
B.	BASILICANUS.	Vatican.	X.	A copy of C, except a gap which was filled up from D.
F.	AMBROSIANUS.	Milan.	IX or X.	Andria wanting.
E.	RICCARDIANUS.	Florence.	XI.	Andria 1–39 wanting.
D.	VICTORIANUS.	Vatican.	IX or X.	Also known as C. Laurentianus.
G.	DECURTATUS.	Vatican.	XI or XII.	Much mutilated.
V.	FRAGMENTUM VINDOBONENSE.	Vienna.	X or XI.	Six sheets containing Andria 912–981.

The Bembine is by far the most important, not merely on account of its antiquity, but because it alone has escaped the recension of Calliopius in the seventh century. Codex **A** was in bad condition, as its owner Cardinal Bembo testified, before the end of the fifteenth century. Andria 1–786 is now entirely wanting, and of Adelphi 914–997 only a few letters are legible.

It bears a note written by Politian (1493 A.D.) to the effect that he never saw so old a Codex. The hands of two correctors can be discerned: one of ancient date, which only appears twice in the Andria, and never in the Phormio or Adelphi; the other [1], about the fifteenth century, which changed and added characters in a 'downright shameless fashion.' But, where not thus tampered with, Codex **A** possesses an authority sufficient to outweigh all the other MSS. taken together, though the scribe was not a very careful one, and not unfrequently made palpable mistakes in copying. The later MSS. were so much altered by the Calliopian recension that their independent authority is not very great. In all MSS., even in **A**, the spelling has been much modernised.

The evidence of the MSS. is to some extent supplemented by quotations of ancient writers, and the commentaries of grammarians.

Of these latter, the most important is Aelius Donatus, tutor of St. Jerome, about 350 A.D., and the author of a celebrated grammatical treatise which became the common text-book of mediaeval schools. Priscian (480? A.D.), Servius (about 420 A.D.) in his notes on Vergil, and other more obscure scholiasts are of occasional service.

---

[1] N.B.—The readings of the late corrector of A are indicated in the notes by A_2.

P. TERENTI
PHORMIO.

INCIPIT · TERENTI · PHORMIO ·
ACTA · LVDIS · ROMANIS ·
L · POSTVMIO · ALBINO · L · CORNELIO ·
MERVLA ·
AEDILIBVS · CVRVLIBVS ·
EGERE ·
L · AMBIVIVS · TVRPIO · L · ATILIVS ·
PRAENESTINVS ·
MODOS · FECIT ·
FLACCVS · CLAVDI · TIBIIS · INPARIBVS · TOTA ·
GRAECA · APOLLODORV · EPIDICAZOMENOS ·
FACTA · IIII ·
C · FANNIO · M · VALERIO · COS ·

PERSONAE.

DAVOS SERVOS
GETA SERVOS
ANTIPHO ADVLESCENS
PHAEDRIA ADVLESCENS
DEMIPHO SENEX
PHORMIO PARASITVS
HEGIO
CRATINUS } ADVOCATI
CRITO
DORIO MERCATOR
CHREMES SENEX
SOPHRONA NVTRIX
NAVSISTRATA MATRONA.

PHORMIO.

PROLOGVS.

Postquám poëta vétŭs poëtam nón potest
Retráhere ab studio et trádere hominem in ótium,
Maledíctis deterrére ne scribát parat:
Qui ita díctitat, quas ántehac fecit fábulas,
Tenui ésse oratióne et scripturá levi: 5
Quia núsquam insanum scrípsit adulescéntulum
Cervám videre fúgere et sectarí canes
Et eám plorare, oráre ut subveniát sibi.
Quod si íntellegeret, quóm stetīt olím nova,
Actóris opera mágĭs stetisse quám sua, 10
Minŭs múlto audacter, quám nunc laedit, laéderet.
Nunc sí quis est, qui hoc dícat aut sic cógitet:
'Vetŭs sí poëta nón lacessissét prior,
Nullum ínvenire prólogum possét novos,
Quem díceret, nisi habéret cui male díceret:' 15
Is síbi responsum hoc hábeat, in medio ómnibus
Palmam ésse positam, qui ártem tractent músicam.
Ille ád famem hunc ab stúdio studuit refcere:
Hic réspondere vóluit, non lacéssere.
Benedíctis si certásset, audissét bene: 20
Quod ab íllo adlatum est, íd sibi rellatúm putet.
De illó iam finem fáciam dicundí mihi,
Peccándi quom ipse dé se finem nón facit.
Nunc quíd velim animum atténdite. adportó novam
Epídicazomenon quám vocant comoédiam 25

Graecí, Latini Phórmionem nóminant:
Quia prímas partis quí aget, is erit Phórmio
Parasítus, per quem rés geretur máxume,
Volúntas vostra si ád poëtam accésserit.
Date óperam, adeste aequo ánimo per siléntium, 30
Ne símili utamur fórtuna, atque usí sumus
Quom pér tumultum nóster grex motús loco est:
Quem actóris virtus nóbis restituít locum
Bonitásque vostra adiútans atque aequánimitas.

ACTUS I.

SC. 1.

DAVOS.

(*Athens: a place where four streets meet. The houses of Demipho and Chremes open on to the stage, and Dorio's house is supposed to be within sight. The scene is unchanged throughout the Play.*) *Enter Davus from the Forum, holding in his hand a purse of brown leather. He addresses the audience.*

Amícus summus méus et popularís Geta   35
Heri ád me venit. érat ei de ratiúncula
Iam prídem apud me rélicuom pauxíllulum
Nummórum : id ut confícerem : confeci : ádfero. (*displaying the purse.*)
Nam erílem filium éius duxisse aúdio   5
Vxórem : ei, credo, múnus hoc (*jingling the money.*) conráditur.   40
(*speaking with some warmth.*) Quam iníque comparátum est,
    ii qui mínus habent
Vt sémper aliquid áddant ditióribus!
Quod ílle únciatim víx de demensó suo,
Suóm defrudans génium, compersít miser,   10
Id ílla únivorsum abrípiet, haud exístumans   45
Quantó labore pártum. porro autém Geta
Feriétur alio múnere, ubi era pépererit :

Porro aútem alio, ubi erit púero natalís dies:
Vbi ínitiabunt. ómne hoc mater aúferet: 15
Puĕr caúsa erit mittúndi. (*The door of Demipho's house opens.*)
    sed videón Getam? 50

SC. 2.

GETA. DAVOS.

(*Enter Geta, not seeing Davus; he turns to speak through the door of Demipho's house to someone within.*)

GE. Si quís me quaeret rúfus—**DA.** (*clapping Geta on the shoulder.*) Praesto est, désine. **GE.** (*bluntly.*) Oh!
At ego óbviam conábar tibi, Dave. **DA.** Áccipe: (*giving the purse to Geta, who weighs it in his hand doubtfully.*) hem!
Lectúm est; conveniet númerus quantum débui.
GE. (*shaking Davus by the hand.*) Amó te: et non negléxisse habeo grátiam.
DA. Praesértim ut nunc sunt móres: adeo rés redit: 5 55
Si quís quid reddit, mágna habenda est grátia.
(*noticing that Geta seems uneasy and anxious.*) Sed quíd tu es tristis? **GE.** Égone? nescis quo ín metu,
Quanto ín periclo símus. **DA.** Quid ístuc ést? **GE.** Scies,
Modo út tacere póssis. **DA.** Abí sis, ínsciens:
Quoius tú fidem in pecúnia perspéxeris, 10 60
Verére verba ei crédere? ubi quid míhi lucri est
Te fállere? **GE.** Ergo auscúlta. **DA.** Hanc operam tíbi dico.
GE. Senís nóstri, Dave, frátrem maiorém Chremem Nostín? **DA.** Quid ni? **GE.** Quid? éius gnatum Phaédriam?

DA. Tam quám te. **GE.** Evenit sénibus ambobús
  simul 15 65
Iter ílli iň Lemnum ut ésset, nostro in Cíliciam
Ad hóspitem antiquom: ís senem per epístulas
Pelléxit, modo non móntis auri póllicens.
DA. Quoi tánta erat res ét supererat? **GE.** Désinas:
Sic ést ingenium. **DA.** (*with an attempt at great dignity.*)
  O! régem me esse opórtuit. 20 70
GE. Abeúntes ambo hic túm senes me fíliis
Relínquont quasi magístrum. **DA.** O Geta! provínciam
Cepísti duram. **GE.** Mi úsus venit, hóc scio:
Meminí relinqui mé deo irató meo.
Coepi ádvorsari primo: quid verbís opu'st? 25 75
Sení fidelis dúm sum, scapulas pérdidi. (*rubbing his shoulders.*)
DA. Venére in mentem mi ístaec: namque inscítia est
Advórsum stimulum cálces! **GE.** Coepi eis ómnia
Facere, óbsequi quae véllent. **DA.** Scisti utí foro.
GE. Nostér mali nil quícquam primo: (*pointing to Chremes'
  house.*) hic Phaédria 30 80
Contínuo quandam náctus est puéllulam,
Citharístriam: hanc amáre coepit pérdite.
Ea hómini serviébat inpuríssumo:
Neque quód daretur quícquam: id curaránt patres.
Restábat aliud níl nisi oculos páscere, (*caricaturing the
  attitudes and movements of the love-sick youth.*) 35 85
Sectári, in ludum dúcere et reddúcere.
Nos ótiosi operám dabamus Phaédriae.
In quo haéc discebat lúdo, exadvorsum ílico
Tonstrína erat quaedam, híc solebamús fere
Plerúmque eam opperíri, dum inde irét domum. 40 90
Intérea dum sedémus illi, intérvenit
Aduléscens quidam lácrumans: nos mirárier.

Rogámus quid sit : (*with dramatic intonation and gestures.*)
'númquam aeque,' inquit, 'ác modo
Paupértas mihi onus vísum est et miserum ét grave.
Modo quándam vidi vírginem hic vicíniae   45 95
Miseram, suam matrem lámentari mórtuam :
Ea síta erat exadvórsum, neque ílli bénevolens
Neque nótus neque cognátus extra unam ániculam
Quisquam áderat, qui adiutáret funus. míseritum est.
Virgo ípsa facie egrégia.' Quid verbís opu'st?   50 100
Commórat omnis nós. ibi continuo Ántipho,
'Voltísne eamus vísere?' alius 'cénseo :
Eámus : duc nos sódes.' imus, vénimus,
Vidémus : virgo púlchra : et quo magis díceres,
Nil áderat adiuménti ad pulchritúdinem :   55 105
Capíllus passus, núdus pes, ipsa hórrida,
Lacrumaé, vestitus túrpis : ut, ni vís boni
In ípsa inesset fórma, haec formam extínguerent.
Ille qui íllam amabat fídicinam tantúmmodo,
'Satis,' ínquit, 'scita est :' nóster vero— **DA.** (*interrupting.*)
        Iám scio :   60 110
Amáre coepit. **GE.** Scín quam? quo evadát vide.
Postrídie ad anum récta pergit : óbsecrat,
Vt eám sibi liceat vísere. illa enim sé negat,
Neque eum aéquom aït facere : íllam civem esse Átticam
Bonám bonis prognátam : si uxorém velit,   65 115
Lege íd licere fácere : sin alitér, negat.
Nostér, quid ageret, néscire : et íllam dúcere
Cupiébat et metuébat absentém patrem.
DA. Non, sí redisset, eí pater veniám daret?
GE. Ille índotatam vírginem atque ignóbilem   70 120
Daret ílli? numquam fáceret. **DA.** Quid fit dénique?
GE. Quid fíat? est parasítus quidam Phórmio,

Homó confidens: (*with sudden vehemence.*) qui íllum di omnes
   pérduint!
DA. Quid ís fécit? GE. Hoc consílium quod dicám dedit:
(*Geta imitates Phormio's voice and manner.*) 'Lex ést ut orbae,
   quí sunt genere próxumi,   75 125
Eis núbant, et íllos dúcere eadem haec léx iubet.
Ego té cognatum dícam et tibi scribám dicam:
Patérnum amicum me ádsimulabo vírginis:
Ad iúdices veniémus: qui fuerít pater,
Quae máter, qui cognáta tibi sit, ómnia haec   80 130
Confíngam, quod erit míhi bonum atque cómmodum.
Quom tu hórum nil refélles, vincam scílicet.
Pater áderit. mihi parátae lites: quíd mea?
Illá quidem nostra erít.' DA. Ioculárem audáciam!
GE. Persuásum est homini: fáctum est: ventum est: víncimur: 85 135
Duxít. DA. Quid narras? GE. Hóc quod audis. DA. Ó
   Geta!
Quid té futurum est? GE. Néscio hercle: unum hóc scio.
Quod fórs feret, ferémus aequo animó. DA. Placet:
   (*patting Geta on the back.*)
Hem! istúc viri est offícium. GE. In me omnis spés mihi
   est.
DA. Laudo. GE. Ád precatorem ádeam credo, quí mihi 90 140
Sic óret: 'nunc amítte quaeso hunc: céterum
Posthác si quicquam, níl precor.' tantúmmodo
Non áddit: 'ubi ego hinc ábiero, vel óccídito.'
DA. Quid paédagogus ílle, qui citharístriam? (*imitating
   Geta's action at 86.*)
Quid reí gerit? GE. Sic, ténuiter. DA. Non múltum
   habet   95 145
Quod dét fortasse? GE. Ímmo nil nisi spém meram.

DA. Pater éius rediit án non? **GE.** Nondum. **DA.** Quíd?
    senem
Quoad éxpectatis vóstrum? **GE.** Non certúm scio:
Sed epístulam ab eo adlátam esse audiví modo
Et ăd pórtitores ésse delatam: hánc petam.   100 150
DA. Num quíd, Geta, aliud mé vis? **GE.** Vt bene sít tibi.
    (*exit Davus towards the Forum. Geta goes to the
    door of Demipho's house and calls.*)
Puer heús! nemon huc pródit? (*there comes to the door a
    slave, to whom Geta hands the purse.*) cape, da hoc
    Dórcio. (*exit towards the Peiraeus.*)

SC. 3.

ANTIPHO. PHAEDRIA.

(*Antipho follows Phaedria out of Demipho's house.*)
AN. Ádeon rem redísse, ut qui mihi cónsultum optumé
    velit esse,
Phaédria, patrem ut éxtimescam, ubi ĭn méntem eius ad-
    ventí venit!
Quód ni fuissem incógitans, ita éxpectarem, ut pár fuit. 155
PH. Quíd istuc? **AN.** Rogitas? quí tam audacis fácinoris
    mihi cónscius sis?
Quód utinam ne Phórmioni id suádere in mentem ínci-
    disset,   5
Neú me cupidum eo ínpulisset, quód mihi principiúm est
    mali?
Nón potitus éssem: fuisset tum íllos mi aegre aliquót dies:
At nón cotidiána cura haec ángeret animum—**PH.** Aúdio. 160
AN. dum expécto quam mox véniat qui hanc mihi ádimat
    consuetúdinem.

PH. Aliís quia defit quód amant aegre est: tíbi quia super-
ést dolet. 10
Amóre abundas, Ántipho.
Nam túa quidem hercle cérto vita haec éxpetenda optán-
daque est.
Ita mé di bene ament, út mihi liceat tám diu quod amó
frui, 165
Iam dépecisci mórte cupio; tú conicito cétera,
Quid ego éx hac inopiá nunc capiam, et quíd tu ex istac
cópia, 15
Vt ne áddam, quod sine súmptu ingenuam, líberalem
náctus es,
Quod habés, ita ut voluísti, uxorem síne mala famá
palam:
Beátus, ni unum désit, animus quí modeste istaéc
ferat. 170
Quod sí tibi res sit scélere cum illo quó mihi est, tum
séntias.
Ita plérique omnes súmus ingenio, nóstri nosmet paéni-
tet. 20
AN. At tú mihi contra núnc videre fórtunatus, Phaédria,
Quoi de íntegro est potéstas etiam cónsulendi, quíd velis:
Retinére, amare, amíttere: ego in eum íncidi infelíx
locum, 175
Vt néque mihi sit ámittendi néc retinendi cópia. (*He turns
to go, when he catches sight of Geta running towards
them.*)
Sed quíd hŏc est? videon égo Getam curréntem huc ad-
veníre? 25
Is ĕst ípsus: ei! timeó miser, quam hic núnc mihi
nuntiét rem.

SC. 4.

GETA. ANTIPHO. PHAEDRIA.

(*Antipho and Phaedria retire to the back of the stage, so that Geta comes hastily on without seeing them.*)

GE. (*evidently much perturbed.*) Núllus es, Getá, nisi iam áliquod tibi consílium celere réperis:
Íta nunc inparátum subito tánta te inpendént mala : 180
Quae néque uti devitém scio neque quó modo me inde éxtraham :
Nam nón potest celári nostra diútius iam audácia. 4
AN. (*apart.*) Quidnam ílle commotús venit? 6
GE. Tum témporis mihi púnctum ad hanc rem est: érus adest. AN. (*apart.*) Quid íllúc mali est?
GE. Quód quom audierit, quód ëius remedium ínveniam iracúndiae? 185
Lóquar? incendam: táceam? instigem: púrgem me? laterém lavem.
Heú me miserum! quóm mihi paveo, tum Ántipho me excrúciat animi: 10
Eíus me miseret, eí nunc timeo, is núnc me retinet: nam ábsque eo esset,
Récte ego mihi vidíssem et senis essem últus iracún diam :
Áliquid convasássem atque hinc me cónicerem protinam ín pedes. 190
AN. (*apart.*) Quam híc fugam aut furtúm parat?
GE. (*meditatively.*) Sed ubi Ántiphonem réperiam? aut qua quaérere insistám via? 15
PH. (*apart.*) Te nóminat. AN. (*apart.*) Nesció quod magnum hoc núntio expectó malum.

PH. (*apart.*) Ah! sánun es? GE. Domum íre pergam:
ibi plúrimum est. (*turns towards Demipho's house.*)
PH. (*apart.*) Revocémus hominem. AN. (*imperiously.*) Sta
ílico. GE. (*without looking round.*) Hem! satís
pro inperio, quísquis es. 195
AN. Geta. GE. (*turning at the sound of his name.*) Ípse
est quem volui óbviam.
AN. (*anxiously.*) Cédo quid portas, óbsecro, atque id, sí
potes, verbo éxpedi.
GE. Fáciam. AN. Eloquere. GE. Módo apud portum—
AN. (*interrupting in a horror-struck voice.*)
Meúmne? GE. Intellexti. AN. Óccidi! PH
(*in surprise.*) Hem! 20
AN. (*in a tone of despair.*) Quíd agam? PH. (*to Ge.*) Quid
aïs? GE. Huíus patrem vidísse me, patruóm tuom
AN. Nám quod ego huic nunc súbito exitio rémedium in·
veniám miser? 200
Quód si eo meae fortúnae redeunt, Phánium, abs te ut
dístrahar,
Núlla est mihi vita éxpetenda. (*he bursts into tears and
buries his face in his hands.*) GE. Ergo ístaec quom
ita sint, Ántipho,
Tánto magís te advígilare aequom est: (*laying his hand on
Antipho's shoulder.*) fórtis fortuna ádiuvat. 25
AN. (*speaking through his sobs.*) Nón sum apud me. GE.
Atqui ópus est nunc quom máxume ut sis,
Ántipho:
Nám si senserít te timidum páter esse, arbitrábitur 205
Cómmeruisse cúlpam. PH. Hoc verum est. AN. (*hope-
lessly.*) Nón possum inmutárier.
GE. Quíd faceres, si aliúd quid gravius tíbi nunc faciun-
dúm foret?

D 2

AN. Quom hóc non possum, illúd minŭs possem. **GE.**
(*impatiently.*) Hoc nîl est, Phaedria: ílicet.   30
Quíd hîc conterimus óperam frustra? quín abeo? **PH.** Et
quidem ego? (*both turn to go.*) **AN.** (*detaining
them and speaking imploringly.*) Óbsecro,
Quíd si adsimulo? (*he strikes a posture.*) sátin est? **GE.**
(*contemptuously.*) Garris. **AN.** Vóltum contemplá-
mini: (*trying to assume a nonchalant air.*) em!   210
Sátine sic est? **GE.** (*decidedly.*) Nón. **AN.** (*making a
great effort to subdue his agitation.*) Quid si sic?
GE. (*surveying him critically.*) Própemodum. **AN.**
(*holding up his head and folding his arms.*) Quid síc?
GE. Sat est:
Ém! istuc serva: et vérbum verbo, pár pari ut respóndeas,
Né te iratus suís saevidicis díctis protelét. **AN.** (*doubtfully.*) Scio.   35
GE. Ví coactum te ésse invitum—**PH.** Lége, iudició.
GE. Tenes?
(*after looking down the street leading to the Peiraeus.*) Séd
quis hîc est senéx, quem video in última platea?
AN. (*after a hurried glance his courageous attitude
instantly vanishes.*) Ípsus est.   215
Non póssum adesse. (*he begins to run away in the opposite
direction.*) **GE.** (*calling after him.*) Ah! quíd agis?
quo abis, Ántipho?
Mane, ínquam. **AN.** (*turning round as he leaves the stage.*)
Egomet me nóvi et peccatúm meum:
Vobís commendo Phánium et vitám meam. (*exit.*)   40
(*Phaedria and Geta look at one another in silence for a moment;
then Phaedria, shrugging his shoulders, begins.*)
PH. Geta, quíd nunc fiet? **GE.** Tú iam litis aúdies:

Ego pléctar pendens, nísi quid me feféllerit. 220
Sed quód modo hic nos Ántiphonem mónuimus,
Id nósmet ipsos fácere oportet, Phaédria.
PH. Aufér mi 'oportet': quín tu, quid faciam, ínpera. 45
GE. Meminístin, olim ut fúerit vostra orátio
In re íncipiunda ad défendendam nóxiam, 225
Iustam íllam causam, fácilem, vincibilem, óptumam?
PH. Memini. **GE.** Ém! nunc ipsa est ópus ea, aut, si quíd potest,
Melióre et callidióre. **PH.** Fiet sédulo. 50
GE. Nunc príor adito tu, égo in insidiis híc ero
Subcénturiatus, sí quid deficiás. **PH.** Age. (*both retire to the back of the stage.*) 230

SC. 5. [II. 1.]

DEMIPHO. GETA. PHAEDRIA.

(*Demipho enters from the Peiraeus, dressed in travelling cloak and hat, evidently in a state of considerable excitement. He does not see Phaedria and Geta.*)

DE. (*indignantly.*) Ítane tandem uxórem duxit Ántipho iniussú meo?
Néc meum inperium—ac mítto inperium—nón simultatém meam
Reveréri saltem! nón pudere! o fácinus audax, ó Geta
Monitór! (*shaking his stick.*) **GE.** (*apart, sarcastically.*) Vix tandem. **DE.** Quíd mihi dicent aút quam causam réperient?
Demíror. **GE.** (*apart.*) Atqui réperiam: aliud cúra. **DE.** An hoc dicét mihi: 5 235

(*in a whining tone.*) 'Invítus feci : léx coëgit'? (*impatiently.*)
audio, fateór. GE. (*apart.*) Places.
DE. Verúm scientem, tácitum causam trádere advorsáriis,
Etiámne id lex coëgit? PH. (*apart.*) Illud dúrum. GE.
(*apart.*) Ego expediám : sine.
DE. Incértum est quid agam, quía praeter spem atque ín-
credibile hoc mi óbtigit :
Ita sum ínritatus, ánimum ut nequeam ad cógitandum
instítuere. (*paces irritably backwards and for-
wards.*)   10 240
Quamobrem ómnis, quom secúndae res sunt máxume, tum
máxume
Meditári secum opórtet, quo pacto ádvorsam aerumnám ferant.
Perícla, damna, exília peregre rédiens semper cógitet,
Aut fíli peccatum aút uxoris mórtem aut morbum fíliae,
Commúnia esse haec, fíeri posse, ut né quid animo sít
novom :   15 245
Quidquíd praeter spem evéniet, omne id députare esse ín
lucro.
GE. (*apart, with mock admiration.*) O Phaédria, incredíbile
est quantum erum ánte-eo sapiéntia.
(*with a caricature of Demipho's tones and gestures.*) Meditáta
mihi sunt ómnia mea incómmoda, erus si ré-
dierit :
Moléndum usque in pistríno, vapulándum, habendae
cómpedes,
Opŭs rúri faciundum : hórum nil quicquam áccidet animó
novom.   20 250
Quidquíd praeter spem evéniet, omne id députabo esse ín
lucro.
Séd quid cessas hóminem adire et blánde in principio
ádloqui ? (*Phaedria advances.*)

DE. Phaédriam mei frátris video fílium mi ire óbviam.
PH. (*effusively holding out both hands.*) Mi pátrue, salve!
    DE. (*shortly.*) Sálve! sed ubi est Ántipho?
PH. Salvóm venire—**DE.** (*interrupting impatiently.*) Crédo:
    hoc respondé mihi.   25 255
PH. Valet, (*pointing to the house.*) híc est: sed satin ómnia
    ex senténtia?
DE. (*gruffly.*) Vellém quidem. **PH.** (*innocently.*) Quid ïstúc
    est? **DE.** (*bursting out passionately.*) Rogitas,
    Phaédria?
Bonás me absente hic cónfecistis núptias.
PH. (*with affected wonder.*) Eho! an íd suscenses núnc
    illi? **GE.** (*apart, rubbing his hand with glee behind
    Demipho's back.*) O artificém probum!
DE. Egon ílli non suscénseam? ipsum géstio   30 260
Darí mi ín conspectum, núnc sua culpa út sciat
Leném patrem illum fáctum me esse acérrumum.
PH. Atquí nil fecit, pátrue, quod suscénseas.
DE. Ecce aútem similia ómnia: omnes cóngruont:
Vnúm quom noris, ómnis noris. **PH.** Haúd ita est. 35 265
DE. Híc ïn nóxia est, ïlle ăd défendendam caúsam adest:
Quom ille ést, hic praesto est: trádunt operas mútuas.
GE. (*aside.*) Probe hórum facta inprúdens depinxít senex.
DE. Nam ni haéc ita essent, cum íllo haud stares, Phaé-
    dria.
PH. (*in a tone of quiet remonstrance.*) Si est, pátrue, culpam
    ut Ántipho in se admíserit,   40 270
Ex quá re minŭs rei fóret aut famae témperans,
Non caúsam dico quín quod meritus sít ferat.
Sed sí quis forte málitia fretús sua
Insídias nostrae fécit adulescéntiae
Ac vícit, nostran cúlpa ea est an iúdicum,   45 275

Qui saépe propter ínvidiam adimunt díviti,
Aut própter misericórdiam addunt paúperi?
GE. (*aside.*) Ni nóssem causam, créderem vera húnc
  loqui.
DE. An quísquam iudex ést, qui possit nóscere
Tua iústa, ubi tute vérbum non respóndeas,   50 280
Ita ut ílle fecit? **PH.** Fúnctus adulescéntuli est
Offícium liberális: postquam ad iúdices
Ventúm est, non potuit cógitata próloqui:
Ita eúm tum timidum ibi óbstupēfecít pudor.
GE. (*aside.*) Laudo húnc: sed cesso adíre quam primúm
  senem? (*advances and bows low to Demipho.*) 55 285
Ere, sálve: salvom te ádvenisse gaúdeo. **DE.** (*raising his
  stick threateningly, whereat Geta keeps at a safe
  distance.*) Oh!
Bone cústos, salve! cólumen vero fámiliae,
Quoi cómmendavi fílium hinc abiéns meum.
GE. (*in a tone of injured innocence.*) Iam dúdum te omnis
  nós accusare aúdio
Inmérito, et me horunc ómnium inmeritíssumo: 60 290
Nam quíd me in hac re fácere voluistí tibi?
Servom hóminem causam oráre leges nón sinunt,
Neque téstimoni díctio est. **DE.** Mitto ómnia.
Do istúc, 'inprudens tímuit adulescéns': sino
'Tu sérvos': verum sí cognata est máxume,   65 295
Non fuít necesse habére: sed id quod léx iubet,
Dotém daretis; quaéreret aliúm virum.
Qua rátione inopem pótius ducebát domum?
GE. Non rátio, verum arguéntum deerat. **DE.** (*sulkily.*)
  Súmeret
Alicúnde. **GE.** (*ironically.*) Alicunde! níl est dictu fá-
  cilius.   70 300

DE. Postrémo, si nullo álio pacto, faénore.
GE. (*with great sarcasm.*) Hui! díxti pulchre: sí quidem quisquam créderet
Te vívo. **DE.** (*angrily.*) Non, non síc futurum est: nón potest.
Egon íllam cum illo ut pátiar nuptam unúm diem?
Nil suáve meritum est. hóminem commonstrárier ;5 305
Mi istúm volo, aut ubi hábitet demonstrárier.
GE. Nĕmpe Phórmionem? **DE.** Istúm patronum múlieris.
GE. Iam fáxo hic aderit. **DE.** Ántipho ubi nunc ést?
GE. Foris.
DE. Abī, Phaédria, eum requíre atque adduc húc. **PH.** Eo:
Rectá via quidem ílluc. (*exit, with a wink at Geta.*) **GE.**
(*apart to Phaedria as he passes.*) Nempe ad Pámphilam. (*exit Geta towards the Forum, with a mocking gesture behind Demipho's back.*) 80 310
DE. Ego deós penatis hínc salutatúm domum
Devórtar: inde ibo ád forum atque aliquót mihi
Amícos advocábo, ad hanc rem qui ádsient,
Vt ne ínparatus sím, si adveniat Phórmio. (*exit into his house.*)

ACTVS II.

SC. 1 [2].

PHORMIO. GETA.

(*Phormio and Geta come on from the Forum, conversing as they walk.*)

PH. Ítane patris aís adventum véritum hinc abiisse? GE. Ádmodum. 315
PH. Phánium relíctam solam? GE. Síc. PH. Et iratúm senem?
GE. Óppido. PH. (*turning away from Geta and speaking to himself.*) Ad te súmma solum, Phórmio, rerúm redit :
Túte hoc intristí : tibi omne est éxedendum : accíngere. (*folding his arms in thought.*)
GE. Óbsecro te. PH. (*to himself, paying no attention to Geta.*) Sí rogabit—GE. Ín te spes est. PH. (*to himself.*) Éccere! 5
Quíd si reddet? GE. Tu ínpulisti. PH. (*in a satisfied tone.*) Síc, opinor. GE. Súbveni. 320
PH. Cédo senem : iam instrúcta sunt mi in córde consilia ómnia.
GE. Quíd ages? PH. Quid vis, nísi uti maneat Phánium, atque ex crímine hoc
Ántiphonem erípiam, atque in me omnem íram derivém senis?
GE. Ó vir fortis átque amicus. (*Phormio makes a mock deprecating gesture.*) vérum hoc saepe, Phórmio, 10

Véreor, ne istaec fórtitudo in nérvom erumpat dénique.
PH. Ah! 325
Nón ita est: factúm est periclum, iám pedum visá est via.
Quót me censes hómines iam devérberasse usque ád necem,
Hóspites, tum cívis? quo magĭs nóvi, tanto saépius.
Cédo dum, en umquam iniúriarum audísti mihi scriptám
    dicam? 15
GE. Quí istuc? **PH.** Quia non réte accipitri ténditur ne-
    que míluo, 330
Quí male faciunt nóbis: illis quí nil faciunt ténditur,
Quía enim in illis frúctus est, in íllis opera lúditur.
Áliis aliunde ést periclum, unde áliquid abradí potest:
Míhi sciunt nil ésse. dices, 'dúcent damnatúm domum': 20
Álere nolunt hóminem edacem, et sápiunt mea sen-
    téntia, 335
Pró maleficio sí beneficium súmmum nolunt réddere.
GE. Nón potĕst satĭs pro mérito ab illo tíbi referri grátia.
PH. Ímmo enim nemo sátĭs pro merito grátiam regí refert.
Téne asymbolúm venire unctum átque lautum e bálneis, 25
Ótiosum ab ánimo, quom ille et cúra et sumptu ab-
    súmitur! 340
Dúm tibi fit quod pláceat, ille ríngitur; tu rídeas,
Prĭŏr bibas, priór decumbas: céna dubia adpónitur—
GE. Quíd ístuc verbi est? **PH.** Úbi tu dubites quíd sumas
    potíssumum.
Haéc quom rationem íneas (*with unction.*) quam sint suávia
    et quam cára sint, 30
Éa qui praebet, nón tu hunc habeas pláne praesentém
    deum? 345
GE. (*looking round.*) Sénĕx adest: vidé quíd agas: prima
    cóitio est acérruma:
Si eám sustinuerís, postilla iam, út lubet, ludás licet.

SC. 2 [3].

DEMIPHO (cum Advocatis). GETA. PHORMIO.

(*Demipho enters, followed by his three friends, who with ostentatious politeness remain at a short distance from him, and busily take notes during the ensuing interview. Phormio and Geta are at the front of the stage, on one side, with their backs turned, pretending not to notice the new comers.*)

DE. (*to his friends.*) En úmquam quoiquam cóntumeliósius
Audístis factam iniúriam quam haec ést mihi?
Adéste quaeso. GE. (*apart to Phormio.*) Irátus est. PH.
  (*apart.*) Quin tu hóc age.   350
Iam ego húnc agitabo. (*speaking in a loud and indignant tone so as to be overheard by Demipho.*) Pró deum inmortálium!
Negăt Phánium esse hanc síbi cognatam Démipho?   5
Hanc Démipho negat ésse cognatám? GE. Negat.
DE. (*in an undertone to his friends.*) Ipsum ésse opinor dé quo agebam. séquimini. (*they cautiously move somewhat nearer.*)
PH. Neque eíus patrem se scíre qui fuerít? GE. Negat. 355
PH. Quia egéns relicta est mísera, ignoratúr parens,   10
Neglégitur ipsa: víde avaritia quíd facit!
GE. (*with affected indignation.*) Si erum ínsimulabis máli-
  tiae, male aúdies.
DE. (*apart.*) O audáciam! etiam me últro accusatum ád-
  venit.   360
PH. Nam iam ádulescenti níl est quod suscénseam,
Si illúm minŭs norat: quíppe homo iam grándior,   15
Paupér, quoi in opere víta erat, rurí fere
Se cóntinebat: íbi agrum de nostró patre

Coléndum habebat: saépe intelea míhi senex 365
Narrábat se hunc neglégere cognatúm suom:
At quém virum! quem ego víderim in vita óptumum. 20
GE. (*with a sneer.*) Videás te atque illum, ut nárras. PH.
(*angrily.*) I in malám crucem!
Nam ni íta eum existumássem, numquam tám gravis
Ob hănc ínimicitias cáperem in vostram íamiliam, 370
Quam is áspernatur núnc tam inliberáliter.
GE. (*working himself up into a pretended rage.*) Pergín ero
absenti mále loqui, inpuríssume? 25
PH. Dignum aútem hoc illo est. GE. Aín tandem, car-
cér? DE. (*calling.*) Geta.
GE. (*bawling, pretending not to hear Demipho.*) Bonórum
extortor, légum contortór. DE. (*calling more
loudly.*) Geta.
PH. (*in an undertone to Geta.*) Respónde. GE. (*turning
round.*) Quis homo est? (*in a tone of great as-
tonishment.*) éhēm! DE. Tace. GE. Absentí
tibi 375
Te indígnas seque dígnas contumélias
Numquám cessavit dícere. DE. (*impatiently.*) Ohe désine! 30
(*speaking to Phormio with ironical politeness.*) Aduléscens,
primum abs te hóc bona veniá peto,
Si tíbi placere pótis est, mi ut respóndeas:
Quem amícum tuom aïs fuísse istum, explaná mihi, 380
Et quí cognatum mé sibi esse díceret.
PH. (*sarcastically.*) Proinde éxpiscare quási non nosses.
DE. Nóssem? PH. Ita. 35
DE. (*emphatically.*) Ego mé nego: tu, quí aïs, redige in
mémoriam.
PH. Eho tú sobrinum tuóm non noras? DE. (*angrily.*)
Énicas.

Dic nómen. **PH.** Nomen? máxume. (*Phormio stops abruptly and turns away.*) **DE.** (*suspiciously.*) Quid nunc taces? 385
PH. (*aside, much disturbed.*) Perii hércle! nomen pérdidi. **DE.** Hem! quid aís? **PH.** (*apart, in a hasty whisper.*) Geta,
Si méministi id quod ólim dictum est, súbice. (*turning to Demipho with great effrontery.*) hem! 40
Non díco: quasi non nóris, temptatum ádvenis.
DE. (*indignantly.*) Egone aútem tempto? **GE.** (*in a whisper.*) Stílpho. **PH.** Atque adeo quíd mea?
Stilphó est. **DE.** Quem dixti? **PH.** (*shouting the name in Demipho's face.*) Stílphonem inquam : nóveras? 390
DE. Neque égo illum noram néque mi cognatús fuit
Quisquam ístoc nomine. **PH.** (*in a provoking tone.*) Ítane? non te horúm pudet? 45
At sí talentum rém reliquissét decem—
DE. Di tíbi malefaciant! **PH.** prímus esses mémoriter
Progéniem vostram usque áb avo atque atavo próferens. 395
DE. (*doggedly.*) Ita ŭt dícis. ego tum quom ádvenissem, quí mihi
Cognáta ea esset, dícerem: itidem tú face: 50
Cedo quí est cognata? **GE.** (*to Demipho, clapping his hands.*) Eu nóster! recte: (*to Phormio, apart, anxiously.*) heus tú, cave!
PH. (*in a lordly manner.*) Dilúcide expedívi quibus me opórtuit
Iudícibus: tum id si fálsum fuerat, fílius 400
Quor nón refellit? **DE.** (*impatiently.*) Fílium narrás mihi?
Quoius dé stultitia díci ut dignum est nón potest. 55
PH. (*ironically.*) At tú (*with a low bow.*) qui sapiens és magistratús adi,

Iudícium de ea causa álterum ut reddánt tibi:
Quandóquidem solus régnas et solí licet 405
Hic de eádem causa bís iudicium adipíscier.
(*Demipho, completely nonplussed, paces irritably up and down; then with difficulty controlling his anger he again addresses Phormio, who, with Geta, has been richly enjoying his discomfiture.*)
DE. Etsí mihi facta iniúria est, verúmtamen 60
Potiús quam litis sécter aut quam te aúdiam,
Itidem út cognata sí sit, id quod léx iubet
Dotís dare, abduc hánc, minas quinque áccipe. 410
PH. (*laughing loudly.*) Hahahaé! homŏ suavis. DE. Quíd
ĕst? num iniquom póstulo?
An ne hóc quidem ego adipíscar, quod ius públicum
est? 65
PH. (*in a tone of righteous indignation.*) Ităn tándem quaeso,
vírginem quom dúxeris,
Mercédem dare lex iúbet eï atque amíttere?
An, ŭt né quid turpe cívis in se admítteret 415
Proptér egestatem, próxumo iussá est dari,
Vt cum úno aetatem dégeret? quod tú vetas. 70
DE. Ita, próxumo quidem: át nos unde? aut quam ób
rem? PH. (*impatiently.*) Ohe!
'Actum,' áiunt, 'nĕ agas.' DE. Nón agam? immo haud
désinam,
Donéc perfecero hóc. PH. (*scornfully.*) Ineptis. DE. Síne
modo. 420
PH. Postrémo tecum níl rei nobis, Démipho, est:
Tuos ést damnatus gnátus, non tu: (*with mocking emphasis.*) nám tua 75
Praetérierat iam ad dúcendum aetas. DE. Ómnia haec
Illúm putato, quae égo nunc dico, dícere

Aut quídĕm cum uxore hac ípsum prohibebó domo. (*turning on his heel in a rage.*) 425
GE. (*apart.*) Irátus est. PH. Tu tĕ ídem melius féceris.
DE. Itane és paratus fácere me advorsum ómnia, 80
Infélix? PH. (*apart to Geta.*) Metuit híc nos, tamĕtsi sédulo
Dissímulat. GE. (*apart to Phormio.*) Bene habent tíbi principia. PH. (*to Demipho, in a tone of parental advice.*) Quín quod est
Ferúndum fers? tuis dígnum factis féceris, 430
Vt amíci inter nos símus. DE. (*with angry contempt.*) Egon tuam éxpetam
Amícitiam? aut te vísum aut auditúm velim? 85
PH. Si cóncordabis cum ílla, habebis quaé tuam
Senĕctútem oblectet: réspice aetatém tuam.
DE. (*furiously.*) Te obléctet: tibi habe. PH. (*with provoking calmness.*) Mínue vero iram. DE. (*with great emphasis.*) Hóc age: 435
Satĭs iám verborum est: nísi tu properas múlierem
Abdúcere, ego illam eíciam: dixi, Phórmio. (*turning away with an angry stamp.*) 90
PH. (*caricaturing Demipho's tones and gestures.*) Si tu íllam attigeris sécŭs quam dignum est líberam,
Dicám tibi ínpingam grándem: dixi, Démipho. (*turning away with a stamp like Demipho.*)
(*apart to Geta.*) Si quíd opus fuerit, heús, domo me. GE. (*apart.*) Intéllego. (*exit Phormio, rudely pushing aside the friends of Demipho, who shakes his stick at him in impotent rage.*) 440

SC. 3 [4].

DEMIPHO. GETA. HEGIO. CRATINVS. CRITO.

(*Demipho, still agitated by his scene with Phormio, soliloquises irritably.*)

DE. Quantá me cura et sóllicitudine ádficit
Gnatús, qui me et se hisce ínpedivit núptiis!
Neque mi ín conspectum pródit, ut saltém sciam,
Quid de hác re dicat quídve sit senténtiae.
(*turning to Geta.*) Abí, víse redierítne iam an nondúm domum. ; 445
GE. Eó. (*exit into Demipho's house.*) **DE.** (*to his friends, who consult their notes with an important air.*)
Videtis quo ín loco res haéc siet:
Quid agó? dic, Hegio. **HE.** (*with low bows to Demipho and Cratinus.*) Égo? Cratinum cénseo,
Si tíbi videtur. **DE.** Díc, Cratine. **CRA.** (*also bowing.*)
Méne vis?
DE. Te. **CRA.** Ego quae ín rem tuam sint éa velim faciás: mihi
Sic hóc videtur: quód te absente hic fílius   10 450
Egít, restitui in íntegrum aequom est ét bonum :
Et id ínpetrabis. díxi. **DE.** Dic nunc, Hégio.
HE. (*again bowing.*) Ego sédulo hunc dixísse credo : vérum ita est,
Quot hómines tot senténtiae: suos quoíque mos.
(*majestically.*) Mihi nón videtur quód sit factum légibus   1; 455
Rescíndi posse: et túrpe inceptum est. **DE.** Díc, Crito.
CRI. Ego ámplius delíberandum cénseo :
Res mágna est. **HE.** Num quid nós vis? **DE.** (*with*

E

ironical politeness.) DE. Fecistís probe. (*the three advocates bow themselves out.*)
(*despairingly*) Incértior sum múlto quam dudúm. (*re-enter Geta.*) GE. Negant
Redísse. DE. (*speaking to himself.*) Frater ést expectandús
mihi: 20 460
Is quód mihi dederit de hác re consilium, íd sequar.
Percóntatum ibo ad pórtum, quoad se récipiat. (*exit towards Peiraeus.*)
GE. At ego Ántiphonem quaéram, ut quae acta hic sínt sciat.
Sed eccum ípsum video in témpore huc se récipere.

SC. 4. [III. 1.]

ANTIPHO. GETA.

(*Enter Antipho soliloquising, without seeing Geta.*)
AN. Énimvero, Antiphó, multimodis cum ístoc animo es
vítuperandus: 465
Ítane te hinc abísse et vitam tuám tutandam aliís dedisse!
Álios tuam rem crédidisti mágis quam tete animádvorsuros?
Nam út ut erant alia, ílli certe quaé nunc tibi domí est consuleres,
Né quid propter tuám fidem decépta poteretúr mali: 5
Quoíus nunc miserae spés opesque súnt in te uno omnés
sitae. 470
GE. (*advancing.*) Et quídem, ere, nos iam dúdum hic te
absentem íncusamus, qui ábieris.

II. 4. [III. 1.] 8-20. PHORMIO. 67

AN. Te ipsúm quaerebam. **GE.** Séd ea causa níhilo magĭs
defécimus.
AN. (*anxiously.*) Loquere óbsecro: quonam ín loco sunt
rés et fortunaé meae?
Num quíd subolet patrí? **GE.** Nil etiam. **AN.** Ecquíd
spei porro͵est? **GE.** Néscio. **AN.** Ah! 10
GE. Nisi Phaédria haud cessávit pro te eníti. **AN.**
(*feelingly.*) Nil fecít novi. 475
GE. Tum Phórmio itidem in hác re ut aliis strénuom
hominem praébuit.
AN. Quid ĭs fécit? **GE.** Confutávit verbis ádmodum ira-
túm senem.
AN. Eu, Phórmio! **GE.** (*with affected modesty.*) Ego quod
pótui porro. **AN.** Mí Geta, omnis vós amo.
GE. Síc habent princípia sese ut díco: adhuc tranquílla
res est, 15
Mánsurusque pátruom pater est, dum húc adveniat. **AN.**
Quíd eum? **GE.** Vt aibat 480
De eíus consilio sése velle fácere quod ad hanc rem át-
tinet.
AN. Quántum metŭs est míhi, videre huc sálvom nunc
patruóm, Geta!
Nam eíus per unam, ut aúdio, aut vivam aút moriar sen-
téntiam.
GE. Phaédria tibi adést. **AN.** Vbinam? **GE.** Eccum ab
suá palaestra exít foras. 20

SC. 5. [III. 2.]

PHAEDRIA. DORIO. ANTIPHO. GETA.

(*Phaedria and Dorio enter. Dorio's manner throughout is rude and brutal: Phaedria in his agitation does not at first perceive Antipho and Geta.*)

PH. (*imploringly.*) Dório, 485
Audi, óbsecro. DO. (*sullenly.*) Non aúdio. PH. (*laying his hand on Dorio's shoulder.*) Parúmper. DO. (*shaking himself free.*) Quin omítte me.

PH. Aúdi quod dicam. DO. Át enim taedet iam aúdire eadem míliens.

PH. Át nunc dicam quód lubenter aúdias. DO. (*with surly acquiescence.*) Loquere, aúdio.

PH. Néqueo te exoráre ut maneas tríduom hoc? (*Dorio abruptly turns on his heel.*) quo núnc abis?

DO. (*insolently.*) Mirábar si tu míhi quicquam adferrés novi.
AN. (*apart.*) Ei! 490
Hunc hóminem metuo né quid—GE. (*interrupting.*) Suo suát capiti? (*ironically.*) idem ego véreor.

PH. Nondúm mihi credis? DO. Háriolare. PH. Sín fidem do? DO. Fábulae.

PH. Faéneratum istúc beneficium púlchre tibi dicés. DO. Logi.

PH. Créde mihi, gaudébis facto: vérum hercle hoc est. DO. Sómnia.

PH. Éxperire: nón est longum. DO. Cántilenam eandém canis. 10 495

PH. Tú cognatus, tú parens, tu amícus, tu—DO. Garrí modo.

PH. Ádeon ingenio ésse duro te átque inexorábili,

Út neque misericórdia neque précibus mollirí queas!
DO. Ádeon te esse incógitantem atque ínpudentem, Phaédria,
Út phaleratis díctis ducas me, ét meam ductes grátiis! 15 500
AN. (*apart.*) Míseritum est. PH. (*turning away from Dorio
in despair.*) Ei! véris vincor. GE. Quám uterque
est similís sui!
PH. Neque Ántipho alia quom óccupatus ésset sollicitú-
dine,
Tum hoc ésse mi obiectúm malum! AN. (*coming forward.*)
Ah! quid ístuc autem est, Phaédria?
PH. Ó fortunatíssume Antipho! AN. Égone? PH. Quoi
quod amás domi est:
Néc cum huius modi úmquam úsus venit út conflictarís
malo. 20 505
AN. Míhin domi est? immo, íd quod aiunt, aúribus tencó
lupum.
Nám neque quo pacto á me amittam néque uti retineám
scio.
DO. Ípsum istuc mi in hóc est. AN. (*sarcastically to
Dorio.*) Heia! né parum nebuló sies.
(*to Phaedria.*) Núm quid hic confécit? PH. Hicine? quód
homo inhumaníssumus:
Pámphilam meam véndidit. GE. Quid? véndidit? AN.
Ain? véndidit? 25 510
PH. Véndidit. DO. (*with coarse irony.*) Quam indígnum
facinus, áncillam aere emptám meo!
PH. Néqueo exorare út me maneat ét cum illo ut mutét
fidem
Tríduom hoc, dum id quód ěst promissum ab amícis argentum aúfero:
(*turning to Dorio.*) Sí non tum dedero, únam praeterea
hóram ne oppertús sies.

DO. (*putting his hands to his ears.*) Óbtundes? (*Phaedria bursts into tears and buries his face in his hands.*) **AN.** Haud lóngum est id quod órat: exorét sine: 30 515
Ídem hic tibi, quod bónĭ promeritus fúeris, conduplicáverit.
DO. Vérba istaec sunt. **AN.** Pámphilamne hac úrbe privarí sines?
Túm praeterea horúnc amorem dístrahi poterín pati?
DO. (*doggedly.*) Néque ego neque tu. **GE.** (*indignantly.*) Dí tibi omnes íd quod es dignús duint!
DO. Égo te complurís advorsum ingénium meum mensís tuli, 35 520
Póllicitantem et níl ferentem, fléntem: nunc contra ómnia haec
Répperi qui dét neque lacrumet: dá locum melióribus.
AN. (*turning to Phaedria.*) Cérte hercle, ego si sátĭs commemini, tíbi quidem est olím dies,
Quam ád dares huic, praéstituta. **PH.** Fáctum. **DO.** Nŭm ego istúc nego?
AN. Iam éa praeteriit? **DO.** Nón, verum haec eï ántecessit. **AN.** Nón pudet 40 525
Vánitatis? **DO.** (*tapping his open palm.*) Mínume, dum ob rem. **GE.** Stércilinium! **PH.** Dório,
Ítane tandem fácere oportet? **DO.** Síc sum; si placeo, útere.
AN. Síc hunc decipis? **DO.** Ímmo enimvero, Ántipho, hic me décipit:
Nam híc me huius modĭ scíbat esse: ego húnc esse aliter crédidi;
Íste me feféllit: ego isti níhilo sum aliter ác fui. 45 530
Séd ut ut haec sunt, támen hoc faciam: crás mane argentúm mihi

Míles dare se díxit: si mihi príŏr tu attuleris, Phaédria,
Meá lege utar, út sit potior, quí prior ad dandúm est.
(*Dorio walks to the back of the stage, followed by
Phaedria with clasped hands, apparently about to
renew his entreaties, but Dorio gives him no chance,
cutting short his intended prayers by an insolent fare-
well.*) Vale! (*exit.*)

SC. 6. [III. 3.]

PHAEDRIA. ANTIPHO. GETA.

(*Phaedria, in the depths of despair, returns from the back of the
stage wringing his hands, scarcely able to speak, and bursting
into tears at the end of his sentence.*)

PH. Quíd faciam? unde ego núnc tam subito huic ár-
   gentum inveniám miser,
Quoí minus nihilo ést? quod, hĭc si pote fuísset ex-
   orárier   535
Tríduom hoc, promíssum fuerat. (*he hides his face in his
   hands and turns away.*) AN. Ítane hunc patiemúr,
   Geta,
Fíeri miserum, quí me dudum, ut díxti, adiuerit cómiter?
Quín, quom opus est, benefícium rursum eï éxperimur
   réddere?   5
GE. (*doubtfully.*) Scío equidem hoc esse aéquom. AN.
   (*clapping Geta on the back.*) Age ergo, sólus ser-
   vare húnc potes.
GE. Quíd faciam? AN. Inveniás argentum. GE. Cúpio:
   sed id unde, édoce.   540
AN. Páter adest hic. GE. Scío: sed quid tum? AN.
   (*impatiently.*) Ah! díctum sapientí sat est.

GE. Ítane? **AN.** Ita. **GE.** Sane hércle pulchre suádes:
etiam tu hínc abis?
Nón triumpho, ex núptiis tuis sí nil nanciscór mali, 10
Ni étiam nunc me huius caúsa quaerere ín malo iubeás
crucem?
AN. Vérum hic dicit. **PH.** (*plaintively*.) Quíd? ego vobis.
Géta, alienus sum? **GE.** Haúd puto: 545
Séd parŭmne est, quod ómnibus nunc nóbis suscensét
senex,
Ni ínstigemus étiam, ut nullus lócŭs relinquatúr preci?
PH. Álius ab oculís meis illam in ígnotum abducét locum?
hem! 15
(*speaking solemnly and slowly*.) Tum ígitur, dum licét dum-
que adsum, lóquimini mecum, Ántipho,
Cóntemplaminí me. **AN.** (*with some alarm*.) Quam ob
rem? aut quídnam facturú's, cedo? 550
PH. Quóquo hinc asportábitur terrárum, certum est pér-
sequi— (*he completely breaks down and finishes his
sentence through his sobs*.)
Aút perire. (*turning away*.) **GE.** Dí bene vortant quód
agas: pedetemptím tamen.
AN. Vídĕ si quid opis pótĕs adferre huic. **GE.** 'Sí
quid'? quid? **AN.** Quaere, óbsecro: 20
Né quid plus minúsve faxit, quód nos post pigeát, Geta.
GE. (*assuming an attitude of deep thought*.) Quaero. (*he re-
mains some moments buried in thought; then with
sudden elation cries out*.) Salvos ést, ut opinor.
(*with a change of tone*.) Vérum enim metuó
malum. 555
AN. Nóli metuere: úna tecum bóna mala tolerábimus.
GE. (*turning to Phaedria*.) Quántum opus est tibi ărgénti,
loquere. **PH.** Sólae trigintá minae.

GE. Tríginta? (*whistling.*) hui! percára est, Phaedria. **PH.**
(*indignantly.*) Ístaec vero vílis est. 25
GE. (*consolingly.*) Áge age, inventas réddam. **PH.** (*hugging
Geta in his joy.*) O lepidum! **GE.** (*pushing Phae-
dria away.*) Aufér te hinc. **PH.** Iam opus est.
GE. Iám feres:
Séd opus est mihi Phórmionem ad hánc rem adiutorém
dari. 560
PH. Praésto est: audacíssume oneris quídvis inpone, ét
feret:
Sólus est homo amíco amicus. **GE.** Eámus ergo ad eum
ócius.
AN. Núm quid ĕst quod operá mea vobis ŏpŭs sit? **GE.**
Nil: verum ábĭ domum 30
Ét illam miseram, quam égo nunc intus scío ĕsse exani-
matám metu,
Cónsolare. céssas? **AN.** Nil est aéque quod faciám lubens.
(*exit to Demipho's house.*) 565
PH. Quá via istuc fácies? **GE.** Dicam in ítinere: hinc
modo te ámove. (*exeunt hurriedly towards the
Forum.*)

ACTVS III [IV].

SC. 1.

DEMIPHO. CHREMES.

(*Enter Demipho and Chremes from the Peiraeus. The latter wears a travelling cloak and hat.*)
DE. Quid? quá profectus caúsa hinc es Lemnúm, Chreme,
Addúxtin tecum fíliam? **CH.** Non. **DE.** Quíd ita non?
CH. Postquám videt me eius máter esse hic diútius,
Simul aútem non manébat aetas vírginis 570
Meam néglegentiam: ípsam cum omni fámilia 5
Ad mé profectam esse aíbant. **DE.** Quid ílli tám diu
Quaeso ígitur commorábare, ubi id audíveras?
CH. (*with some confusion.*) Pol mé detinuit mórbus. **DE.**
    Vnde? aut quí? **CH.** Rogas?
Senéctus ipsa est mórbus. (*abruptly changing the subject.*)
    sed veníssc eas 575
Salvás audivi ex naúta qui illas véxerat. 10
DE. Quid gnáto obtigerit me ábsente, audistín, Chreme?
CH. Quod quídĕm me factum cónsili incertúm facit.
Nam hanc cóndicionem sí quoi tulero extrário,
Quo pácto aut unde míhi sit, dicundum órdine est. 580
Te míhi fidelem esse aéque atque egomet súm mihi 15
Scibam: ílle, si me aliénus adfiném volet,
Tacébit, dum intercédet familiáritas:
Sin spréverit me, plús quam opus est scitó sciet,
(*lowering his voice and looking round towards his house.*) Vere-
    órque ne uxor áliqua hoc rescíscát mea: 585

III [IV]. 1. 20-2. 14.   *PHORMIO.*   75

Quod sí fit, ut me excútiam atque egrediár domo,   20
Id réstat: nam ego meórum solus súm meus.
DE. Scio ita ésse: et istaec míhi res sollicitúdini est:
Neque défetiscar úsque adeo experírier,
Donéc tibi quod pollícitus sŭm id efféccro.   590
(*both retire to the back of the stage where they remain engrossed in their conversation, not noticing the entrance of Geta or Antipho, Demipho having his back turned and Chremes being immediately beyond him.*)

SC. 2.

GETA. (DEMIPHO. CHREMES.)

(*Geta comes on from the Forum, evidently in good spirits.*)

Ego hóminem callidiórem vidi néminem
Quam Phórmionem. vénio ad hominem, ut dícerem
Argéntum opus esse et íd quo pacto fíeret.
Vixdúm dimidium díxeram, intelléxerat:
Gaudébat: me laudábat: quaerebát senem.   5 595
Dis grátias agébat, tempus síbi dari,
Vbi Phaédriae esse osténderet nihiló minus
Amícum sese quam Ántiphoni. hominem ád forum
Iussi ópperiri: eo me ésse adducturúm senem. (*as he turns towards the house he catches sight of Demipho.*)
Sed ĕccum ípsum. (*peering cautiously round.*) quis ĕst
    ultérior? attat Phaédriae   10 600
Patĕr vénit. sed quid pértimui autem bélua?
An quía quos fallam pro úno duo sunt míhi dati?
Commódius esse opínor duplici spe útier.
Petam hínc unde a primo ínstitui: is si dát, sat est:

Si ab eó nil fiet, tum húnc adoriar hóspitem.   15 605
(*Geta pauses for a few moments in thought, making up his plan
of action, and so does not notice the door of Demipho's house
opening.*)

SC. 3.

ANTIPHO. GETA. CHREMES. DEMIPHO.

(*Antipho speaks his first words as he comes out of the door of
Demipho's house. When Geta, Demipho, and Chremes come
down the stage at v.* 609 *Antipho steals to the back, unseen.*)

AN. Expécto quam mox récipiat sesé Geta.
(*catching sight of Chremes.*) Sed pátruom video cúm patre
    astantem. eí mihi!
Quam tímeo, adventus húius quo impellát patrem.
GE. (*having made up his mind.*) Adíbo. (*approaching
    Chremes and speaking with effusion.*) O salve! nóster
    Chreme. CH. Salvé! Geta.
GE. Veníre salvom vólup est. CH. (*shortly.*) Credo. GE.
    Quíd agitur?   5 610
CH. (*irritably.*) Multa ádvenienti, ut fít, nova hic—com-
    plúria.
GE. Ita. de Ántiphone audístin quae facta? CH. Ómnia.
GE. (*to Demipho.*) Tun díxeras huic? (*with affected indigna-
    tion.*) fácinus indignúm, Chreme,
Sic círcumiri! DE. Id cum hóc agebam cómmodum.
GE. Nam hercle égo quoque id quidem ágitans mecum
    sédulo   10 615
Invéni, opinor, rémedium huic rei. CH. (*eagerly.*) Quid,
    Geta?
DE. Quod rémedium? GE. (*goes between the two old men*

and draws them more forward, speaking in a confidential tone.) Vt abii ábs te, fit forte óbviam
Mihi Phórmio. **CH.** Qui Phórmio? **GE.** Is qui istám --
CH. Scio.
GE. Visúm est mi, ut eius témptarem senténtiam.
Prendo hóminem solum: 'quór non,' inquam, 'Phórmio, 15 620
Vidés, inter nos síc haec potius cúm bona
Vt cómponamus grátia quam cúm mala?
Erŭs líberalis ést et fugitans lítium:
Nam céteri quidem hércle amici omnés modo
Vno óre auctores fuére, ut praecipitem hánc (*pointing to the house where Phanium is.*) daret.' 20 625
AN. (*aside.*) Quid hic coéptat aut quo evádet hodie? **GE.**
'an légibus
Datúrum poenas díces, si illam eiécerit?
Iam id éxploratum est: héia! sudabís satis,
Si cum íllo inceptas hómine: ea eloquéntia est.
Verúm pono esse víctum eum: at tandém tamen 25 630
Non cápitis ei res ágitur, sed pecúniae.'
Postquam hóminem his verbis séntio mollírier,
'Solí sumus nunc hic,' ínquam: 'eho! dic, quid vís dari
Tibi ín manum, ut erus hís desistat lítibus,
Haec hínc facessat, tú molestus né sies?' 30 635
AN. (*aside, greatly alarmed.*) Satin ílli di sunt própitii?
GE. 'nam sát scio,
Si tu áliquam partem aequí bonique díxeris,
Vt ĕst ílle bonus vir, tría non commutábitis
Verba hódie inter vos.' **DE.** Quís te istaec iussít loqui?
CH. Immó, non potuit mélius pervenírier 35 640
Eo quó nos volumus. **AN.** (*aside, despairingly.*) Óccidi!
DE. Perge éloqui.

GE. A prímo homo insaníbat. **CH.** Cedo, quid póstulat?
GE. Quid? nímium quantum lubuit. **CH.** Dic. **GE.** 'Si
quís daret
Taléntum magnum.' **DE.** (*in a rage.*) Immó malum hercle!
ut níl pudet!
GE. Quod díxi ei adeo: 'quaéso, quid si fíliam 40 645
Suam únicam locáret? parvi réttulit
Non súscepisse: invénta est quae dotém petat.'
Vt ăd paúca redeam ac míttam illius inéptias,
Haec dénique eius fuít postrema orátio:
'Ego,' ínquit, 'a princípio amici fíliam, 45 650
Ita ut aéquom fuerat, vólui uxorem dúcere.
Nam míhi veniebat ín mentem eius incómmodum,
In sérvitutem paúperem ad ditém dari.
Sed mi ópus erat, ut apérte tibi nunc fábuler,
Aliquántulum quae adférret, qui dissólverem 50 655
Quae débeo: et etiám nunc, si volt Démipho
Dare quántum ab hac accípio, quae sponsá est mihi,
Nullám mihi malim quam ístanc uxorém dari.'
AN. (*aside.*) Vtrúm stultitia fácere ego hunc an málitia
Dicám, scientem an ínprudentem, incértŭs sum. 55 660
DE. Quid si ánimam debet? **GE.** 'Áger oppositus pígnori
Ob décĕm minas est.' **DE.** (*impatiently.*) Áge age, iam
ducát: dabo.
GE. 'Aedículae item sunt ób decem alias.' **DE.** Oíeï!
Nimiúm est. **CH.** Ne clama: *re*petito hasce a mé decem.
GE. 'Vxóri emunda ancíllula est: tum plúscula 60 665
Supĕlléctile opus est: ópus est sumptu ad núptias:
His rébus pone sáne, inquit, decém minas.'
DE. (*pushing Geta aside violently.*) Sescéntas proinde scrí-
bito iam míhi dicas:
Nil do: ínpuratus me ílle ut etiam inrídeat?

CH. (*trying to calm his brother's anger.*) Quaeso, égo dabo.
quiésce : tu modo fílius   65 670
Fac ut íllam ducat, nós quam volumus.   AN. (*aside, despairingly.*) Eí mihi!
Geta, óccidisti mé tuis falláciis.
CH. Mea caúsa eïcitur: me hóc est aequom amíttere.
GE. 'Quantúm potest me cértiorem,' inquít, 'face,
Si illám dant, hanc ut míttam: ne incertús siem: 70 675
Nam illí mihi dotem iám constituerúnt dare.'
CH. (*nervously.*) Iam accípiat : illis répudium renúntiet :
Hanc dúcat. DE. Quae quidem ílli res vortát male!
CH. Oppórtune adeo argéntum nunc mecum áttuli,
Fructúm quem Lemni uxóris reddunt praédia :   75 680
Inde súmam : uxori tíbi opus esse díxero. (*exeunt Demipho and Chremes into the house of the latter.*)

SC. 4.

ANTIPHO. GETA.

AN. (*calling angrily.*) Geta. GE. Hém! AN. Quid egisti?
GE. (*rubbing his hands with great glee.*) Émunxi
argentó senes.
AN. Satin ést id? GE. Nescio hércle, tantum iússŭs sum.
AN. (*striking him.*) Eho! vérbero! aliud míhi respondes
ác rogo?
GE. (*rubbing his shoulder, and speaking in an injured tone.*)
Quid érgo narras? AN. Quíd ego narrem? operá
tua   685
Ad réstim mihi quidĕm rés redit planíssume.   5
(*with the greatest bitterness.*) Vt té quidem omnes dí deae
superi ínferi

Malís exemplis pérdant! em! si quíd velis,
Huic mándes, qui te ad scópulum e tranquillo aúferat.
Quid mínus utibile fuít quam hoc ulcus tángere 690
Aut nóminare uxórem? iniecta est spés patri 10
Posse íllam extrudi, cédo nunc porro, Phórmio
Dotém si accipiet, úxor ducendá est domum,
Quid fíet? GE. (*testily*.) Non enim dúcet. AN. (*ironically*.)
    Novi. céterum
Quom argéntum repetent, nóstra causa scílicet 695
In nérvom potius íbit? GE. Nil est, Ántipho, 15
Quin méle narrando póssit depravárier.
Tu id quód boni est excérpis, dicis quód mali est.
Audí nunc contra: iám si argentum accéperit,
Ducénda est uxor, út aïs: concedó tibi: 700
Spatiúm quidem tandem ádparandis núptiis, 20
Vocándi, sacrificándi dabitur paúlulum.
Intérea amici, quód polliciti súnt, dabunt:
Inde íste reddet. AN. Quam ób rem? aut quid dicét?
    GE. Rogas?
Quot rés! (*in an oracular tone*.) 'postilla mónstra eveneruńt
    mihi! 705
Introfit in aedis áter alienús canis: 25
Anguís per ínpluvium décidit de tégulis:
Gallína cecinit: ínterdixit háriolus:
Harúspex vetuit ánte brumam aliquíd novi
Negóti incipere, quaé causa est iustíssuma.' 710
Haec ffent. AN. Vt modo fíant! GE. (*confidently*.) Fient:
    mé vide. 30
Pater éxit: abi, dic ésse argentum Phaédriae. (*exit Antipho
    towards the Forum.*)

SC. 5.
DEMIPHO. CHREMES. GETA.

(*Demipho and his brother come out of Chremes' house in conversation. Demipho has in his hand a large bag of money.*)
DE. (*with some impatience.*) Quiétus esto, inquam: égo curabo né quid verborúm duit.
Hoc témere numquam amíttam ego a me, quín mihi testis ádhibeam:
Quoi dem ét quam ob rem dem, cómmemorabo. GE. (*apart, to the audience.*) Vt caútus est, ubi níl opu'st. 715
CH. (*anxiously.*) Atque íta opus facto est: ét matura, dúm lubido eadem haéc manet:
Nam si áltera illaec mágis instabit, fórsitan nos refciat. 5
GE. (*aside.*) Rem ipsám putasti. DE. (*turning to Geta.*) Dúc me ad eum ergo. GE. Nón moror. (*Geta turns to lead the way, but Chremes detains his brother, and speaks in a low tone.*) CH. Vbi hoc égeris,
Transíto ad uxorém meam, ut convéniat hanc priŭs quam hínc abit.
Dicát eam dare nos Phórmioni núptum, ne suscénseat: 720
Et mágis esse illum idóneum, qui ipsí sit familiárior:
Nos nóstro officio nón digressos ésse: quantum is vóluerit 10
Datum ésse dotis. DE. (*impatiently.*) Quíd tua, malum, íd réfert? CH. Magni, Démipho.
Non sátis est tuom te offícium fecisse, íd si non fama ádprobat:
Volo ípsius [quoque] volŭntáte haec fieri, né se eiectam praédicet. 725

F

DE. Idem égo ístuc facere póssum.   CH. Mulier múlieri
  magis cónvenit.
DE. (*yielding with an ill-grace.*) Rogábo. (*exit towards the
  Forum.*) CH. (*meditatively.*) Vbi illas núnc ego
  reperíre possim, cógito. (*he paces slowly towards
  the back of the stage.*)   15

SC. 6. [V. 1.]

SOPHRONA. CHREMES.

(*Sophrona comes out of Demipho's house, not seeing Chremes.
She is in a state of tremulous agitation.*)

SO. Quíd agam? quem mi amícum inveniam mísera? aut
  quo consília haec referam?
Aút unde auxilium petam?
Nám vereor, era ne ób meum suasum indígna iniuria ád-
  ficiatur: 730
Íta patrem adulescéntis facta haec tólerare audió vio-
  lenter.
CH. (*aside, in some surprise.*) Nám quae haec anus est, éx-
  animata a frátre quae egressá est meo?   5
SO. Quod ŭt fácerem egestas me ínpulit, quom scírem
  infirmas núptias
Hasce ésse, ut id consúlerem, interea víta ut in tutó foret.
CH. (*aside, excitedly.*) Cérte edepol, nisi me ánimus fallit
  aút parum prospíciunt oculi,   735
Meaé nutricem gnátae video.   SO. Néque ílle investigátur—
  CH. (*aside.*) Quid ago?
SO. Quí est eius pater.   CH. (*aside.*) Ádeo an maneo, dum
  haéc quae loquitur mágís cognosco?   10

SO. Quód si eum nunc reperíre possim, níl est quod vereár. CH. Ea est ipsa:
Cónloquar. (*advances.*) SO. (*nervously looking every way except the right.*) Quis hic lóquitur?—CH. (*calling softly.*) Sophrona. SO. Ét meum nomen nóminat?
CH. Réspice ad me. SO. (*with a cry of amazement.*) Di, óbsecro vos, éstne hic Stilpho? CH. Nón. SO. (*in consternation.*) Negas? 740
CH. (*pushing her away from his house, and speaking in a low but excited tone.*) Cóncede hinc a fóribus paulum istórsum sodes, Sóphrona.
Ne me ístoc posthac nómine appelléssis. SO. Quid? non óbsecro es 15
Quem sémper te esse díctitasti? CH. (*looking towards his house in manifest alarm.*) St'! SO. Quid has metuís foris?
CH. Conclúsam hic habeo uxórem saevam. (*Sophrona is speechless from terror, and trembles so violently that she can scarcely stand, but Chremes is so excited that he does not notice it.*) vérum istoc me nómine
Eo pérperam olim díxi, ne vos fórte inprudentés foris 715
Effútiretis átque id porro aliqua úxor mea rescísceret.
SO. Istóc pol nos te hic ínvenire míserae numquam pótuimus. 20
CH. Eho! díc mihi, quid reí tibi est cum fámilia hac unde éxis?
Vbi illaé sunt? SO. (*bursting into tears.*) Miseram me! CH. Hém! quid est? vivóntne? SO. (*speaking through her sobs.*) Vivit gnáta.
Matrem ípsam ex aegritúdine hac miserám mors consecúta est. 750

CH. Male fáctum! SO. Ego autem, quae éssem anus desérta, egens, ignóta,
Vt pótui nuptum vírginem locávi huic adulescénti, 25
Harúm qui est dominus aédium. CH. (*with astonishment.*) Antiphónine? SO. Hem! isti ípsi.
CH. (*utterly bewildered.*) Quid? duásne is uxorés? SO. Au! obsecro, únam ille quidem hanc sólam.
CH. (*scarcely believing that it can be true.*) Quid íllam álteram quae dícitur cognáta? SO. Haec ergo est.
CH. Quíd aïs? 755
SO. Compósito factum est, quó modo hanc amáns habere pósset
Sine dóte. CH. (*he turns away, holding up his clasped hands in thankfulness.*) Di vostrám fidem! quam saépe forte témere 30
Evéniunt quae non aúdeas optáre! offendi advéniens,
Quocúm volebam et út volebam, cónlocatam amári:
Quod nós ambo opere máxumo dabámus operam ut fíeret, 760
Sine nóstra cura, máxuma sua cúra haec sola fécit.
SO. (*anxiously recalling Chremes from his soliloquy.*) Nunc quíd opus facto sít vide: pater ádulescentis vénit, 35
Eumque ánimo iniquo hoc óppido ferre áiunt. CH. Nil perícli est.
Sed pér deos atque hómines meam esse hanc cávĕ resciscat quísquam.
SO. Nemo éx me scibit. CH. Séquere *tu* me: cétera intus aúdies. (*exeunt into Demipho's house.*) 765

ACTVS IV.

SC. 1. [V. 2.]

DEMIPHO. GETA.

(*Demipho returns with Geta, after having paid the money to Phormio.*)

DE. Nostrápte culpa fácimus ut malós expediat ésse,
Dum nímium dici nós bonos studémus et benígnos.
Ita fúgias, ne praetér casam, quod áiunt. (*angrily.*) nonne id sát erat,
Accípere ab illo iniúriam? etiam argéntum est ultro obiéctum,
Vt sít qui vivat, dum áliud aliquid flágiti confíciat. 5 770
GE. Planíssume. **DE.** Eis nunc praémium est, qui récta prava fáciunt—
GE. Veríssume. **DE.** ut stultíssume quidem íllí rem gessérimus.
GE. Modo ut hóc consilio póssiet discédi, ut istam dúcat.
DE. (*with a start.*) Etiámne id dubium est? **GE.** Haúd scio hercle, ut homó est, an mutet ánimum.
DE. Hem! mútet autem? **GE.** Néscio: verúm, si forte, díco. 10 775
DE. Ita fáciam, ut frater cénsuit, ut uxórem eius huc addúcam,
Cum ista út loquatur. tú, Geta, abi prae: núntia hanc ventúram. (*exit Demipho into Chremes' house.*)
GE. (*soliloquising.*) Argéntum inventum est Phaédriae: de iúrgio silétur:
Provísum est, ne in praeséntia haec hinc ábeat: quid nunc pórro?

Quid fiet? in eodém luto haesitás: vorsuram sólves, 780
Geta: praésens quod fuerát malum in diem ábiit: plagae
    créscunt,
Nisi próspicis. nunc hínc domum ibo ac Phánium edo-
    cébo,
Ne quíd vereatur Phórmionem aut eíus oratiónem. (*exit
    into Demipho's house.*)

SC. 2. [V. 3.]

DEMIPHO. NAVSISTRATA.

(*Demipho escorts Nausistrata from her house, with studied
politeness.*)

DE. Age dum, út soles, Nausístrata, fac illa út placetur
    nóbis,
Vt suá voluntate íd quod est faciúndum faciat. NA.
    Fáciam. 785
DE. Paritér nunc opera me ádiuves, ac ré dudum opitu-
    láta es.
NA. Factúm volo: (*with spiteful emphasis*.) ac pol mínŭs
    queo virí cúlpa, quam me dígnum est.
DE. Quid aútem? NA. Quia pol meí patris bene párta
    indiligénter 5
Tutátur: nam ex eis praédiis talénta argenti bína
Statím capiebat: vír viro quid praéstat! DE. Binan
    quaéso? 790
NA. Ac rébus vilióribus multó talenta bína. DE. (*with
    an affectation of great surprise.*) Hui!
NA. Quid haéc videntur? DE. Scílicet. NA. (*warmly.*)
    Virúm me natum véllem:

Ego osténderem—DE. Certó scio. NA. quo pácto—DE.
Parce sódes, 10
Vt póssis cum illa, né te adulescens múlier defetíget.
NA. Faciam út iubes: sed meúm virum abs te exíre video.

SC. 3.

CHREMES. DEMIPHO. NAVSISTRATA.

(*Chremes comes quickly out of his brother's house in great excitement. He does not at first see his wife.*)
CH. (*calling to Demipho in an agitated voice.*) Ehĕm, Démipho! 795
Iam illí datum est argéntum? DE. Curavi ílico. CH. Nollém datum.
(*catching sight of Nausistrata.*) Ei! vídeo uxorem: paéne plus quam sát erat. DE. Quor nollés, Chremes?
CH. (*confused.*) Iam récte. DE. Quid tu? ecquid locutu's cum ístac, quam ob rem hanc dúcimus? (15)
CH. Transégi. DE. Quid aït tándem? CH. Abduci nón potest. DE. (*much surprised.*) Qui nón potest?
CH. (*scarcely able to answer in his perplexity.*) Quia utérque utrique est córdi. DE. Quid ístuc nóstra? CH. Magni: praéter haec 800
Cognátam comperi ésse nobis. DE. Quíd? deliras. CH. Síc erit:
Non témere dico: rédii mecum in mémoriam. DE. Satin sánus es?
NA. Au! óbsecro, vidĕ ne ín cognatam pécces. DE. Non est. CH. Né nega: (2)

Patrís nómen aliud díctum est: hoc tu errásti. **DE.** (*incredulously.*) Non norát patrem?
CH. Norát. **DE.** Quor aliud díxit? **CH.** (*apart to Demipho, glancing with terror towards his wife whose suspicions are evidently aroused.*) Numquamne hódie concedés mihi, 10 805
Neque intélleges? **DE.** Si tú nil narras? **CH.** (*impatiently.*) Pérdis. **NA.** Miror quíd siet.
DE. Equidem hércle nescíó. **CH.** (*desperately.*) Vin scire? at íta me servet Iúppiter,
Vt própior illi, quăm ego sum ac tu, némo est. **DE.** (*in amazement.*) Di vostrám fidem! (25)
Eámus ad ipsam: una ómnis nos aut scíre aut nescire hóc volo. (*he turns towards the door of his house, beckoning to Chremes and Nausistrata to follow him.*) **CH.** (*stopping Demipho.*) Ah!
DE. Quid ést? **CH.** (*petulantly.*)Ităn parvam míhi fidem esse apúd te! **DE.** (*impatiently.*) Vin me crédere? 15 810
Vin sátis quaesitum mi ístuc esse? age, fíat. quid? illa fília
Amíci nostri quíd futurum est? **CH.** Récte. **DE.** Hanc igitur míttimus?
CH. Quid ni? **DE.** Ílla maneat? **CH.** Síc. **DE.** (*turning to Nausistrata with a shrug of his shoulders.*) Ire igitur tíbi licet, Nausístrata. (30)
NA. Sic pól commodius ésse in omnis árbitror, quam ut coéperas,
Manére hanc; nam perlíberalis vísa est, quom vidí, mihi. (*exit into her house, Demipho holding the door open for her.*) 20 815
DE. (*turning abruptly to his brother.*) Quid istúc negoti est?

CH. (*anxiously*.) Iámne operuit óstium? DE. Iam.
CH. (*Chremes goes to the door, feels that it is fast shut, then leads away the astonished Demipho to the farthest corner of the stage.*) O Iúppiter!
Di nós respiciunt: gnátam inveni núptam cum tuo fílio.
DE. Hem!
Quo pácto potuit? CH. (*looking round nervously*.) Nón satis tutus ést ad narrandum híc locus. (35)
DE. At tu íntro abi. CH. Heus! ne fílii quidem hŏc nóstri resciscánt volo. (*exeunt into Demipho's house.*)

SC. 4.

ANTIPHO.

(*Antipho returns after helping Phaedria to settle matters with Dorio. He is in deep dejection about his own affairs.*)
Laetús sum, ut meae res sése habent, fratri óbtigisse quód
    volt. 820
Quam scítum est, eius modí parare in ánimo cupiditátes,
Quas, quóm res advorsaé sient, pauló mederi póssis!
Hic símul argentum répperit, curá sese expedívit:
Ego núllo possum rémedio me evólvere ex his túrbis, ;
Quin, si hóc celetur, ín metu, sin pátefit, in probró sim. 825
Neque mé demum nunc réciperem, ni mi ésset spes osténta
Huiúsce habendae. séd ubinam Getam ínvenire póssim?
Vt rógem, quod tempus conveniundi pátris me capere
    suádeat.
(*Antipho goes to the back of the stage to look up the street on the left, and so does not see Phormio enter on the right.*)

SC. 5.

PHORMIO. ANTIPHO.

(*Phormio comes on from the Forum, in high spirits.*)
PH. (*to the audience.*) Argéntum accepi, Dórioni sólvi, abduxi múlierem,
Curávi propria ut Phaédria poterétur: nam emissá est manu. 830
Nunc úna mihi res étiam restat quae ést conficiunda, ótium
Ab sénibus ad potándum ut habeam: nam áliquot hos sumám dies.
AN. (*turning round.*) Sed Phórmio est: quid aís? **PH.** Quid?
AN. Quidnam núnc facturu'st Phaédria? 5
PH. Vicíssim partis tuás acturus ést. **AN.** Quas? **PH.** Vt fugitét patrem. 835
Te suás rogavit rúrsum ut ageres, caúsam ut pro se díceres.
Nam pótaturus ést apud me. ego me íre senibus Súnium
Dicam ád mercatum, ancíllulam emptum, dúdum quam dixít Geta: 10
Ne quom híc non videant mé, conficere crédant argentúm suom. (*a knocking is heard within the door of Demipho's house.*)
Sed óstium concrépuit abs te. **AN.** Vídĕ! quis egreditúr?
PH. Geta est. (*both withdraw to the back of the stage.*) 840

SC. 6.

GETA. ANTIPHO. PHORMIO.

(*Geta rushes out of Demipho's house in a state of wild excitement.*)

GE. (*raising his clasped hands aloft.*) Ó Fortuna! O Fórs
Fortuna! quántis commoditátibus,
Quám subito meo ero Ántiphoni ope vóstra hunc onerastís
diem!—
AN. (*apart to Phormio.*) Quídnam hic sibi volt? **GE.** nósque
amicos eíus exonerastís metu!
(*with a sudden change of tone, gathering up the folds of his
cloak.*) Séd ego nunc mihi césso, qui non úmerum
hunc onero pállio,
Átque hominem propero ínvenire, ut haéc quae con-
tigerínt sciat. 5 845
AN. (*apart, greatly astonished.*) Núm tu intellegis, híc quid
narret? **PH.** (*apart.*) Núm tu? **AN.** (*apart.*) Nil.
PH. (*apart.*) Tantúndem ego.
GE. Íre ad Doriónem hinc pergam: ibi núnc sunt. **AN.**
(*calling to Geta who has started to go.*) Heus! Geta.
GE. (*testily, without looking round.*) Ém tibi!
Núm mirum aut novóm est revocari, cúrsum quom institerís?
AN. Geta!
GE. Pérgit hercle: númquam tu odio tuó me vinces. **AN.**
Nón manes?
GE. Vápula. **AN.** (*angrily.*) Id quidém tíbi iam fiet, nísi
resistis, vérbero. 10 850
GE. Fámiliariórem oportet ésse hunc: minitatúr malum.
(*turning round.*)
Séd ísne est quem quaero án non? ipsu'st, cóngredere
actutúm. **AN.** Quid est?

GE. (*in a transport of delight.*) O ómnium, quantúm est qui vivont, hómo hominum ornatíssume:
Nám sine controvórsia ab dis sólus diligere, Ántipho.
AN. Íta velim: sed, quí istuc credam ita ésse, mihi dicí velim.   15 855
GE. Sátin est si te délibutum gaúdio reddo? AN. (*impatiently.*) Énicas.
PH. (*Phormio, who had remained somewhat in the background, now advances.*) Quín tu hinc pollicitátiones aúfer et quod férs cedo. GE. O!
Tú quoque aderas, Phórmio? PH. Aderam: séd tu cessas?
    GE. (*places himself between Antipho and Phormio, and assumes an air of great importance.*) Áccipe, em!
Út modo argentúm tibi dedimus ápŭd forum, rectá domum
Súmŭs profecti: intérea mittit érŭs me ad uxorém tuam.   20 860
AN. Quam ób rem? GE. (*impatient at the interruption.*)
    Omitto próloqui: nam níl ad hanc rem est, Ántipho:
(*Geta enacts the scene which he describes, 862–9, with much vivacity of tone and gesture.*)
Úbi ín gynaeceum íre occipio, púer ad me adcurrít Mida,
Póne adprendit pállio, resupínat: respició, rogo
Quam ób rem retineát me: ait esse vétitum intro ad eram accédere.
'Sóphrona modo frátrem huc,' inquit, 'sénis introduxít Chremem,'   25 865
Eúmque nunc esse íntus cum illis: hóc ubi ego audivi, ád foris
Súspenso gradú placide ire pérrexi, accessi, ástiti,
Ánimam compressi, aúrem admovi: ita ánimum coepi atténdere,

Hóc modo sermónem captans. **AN.** (*clapping his hands.*)
Eú, Geta! **GE.** Hic pulchérrumum
Fácinus audivi: ítaque paene hercle éxclamavi gaúdio. 30 870
AN. Quód? **GE.** Quodnam arbitráre? **AN.** Nescio. **GE.**
Átqui mirificíssumum:
Pátruos tuos est páter inventus Phánio uxorí tuae. **AN.**
(*starts back in utter amazement.*) Hem!
Quíd aïs? **GE.** Cum eius consuévit olim mátre in Lemno
clánculum.
PH. (*incredulously.*) Sómnium! utĭn haec ígnoraret suóm
patrem? **GE.** Aliquid crédito,
Phórmio, esse caúsae: sed me cénsen potuisse ómnia 3; 875
Íntellegere extra óstium, intus quae ínter sese ipsi égerint?
AN. Átque ego quoque ináudivi illam fábulam. **GE.** Immo
etiám dabo
Quó magĭs credas: pátruos interea índe huc egreditúr foras:
Haúd multo post cúm patre idem récipit se intro dénuo:
Aït uterque tíbi potestatem éius adhibendaé dari: 40 880
Dénique ego missús sum, te ut requírerem atque ad-
dúcerem.
AN. (*excitedly.*) Quín ergo rape mé: quid cessas? **GE.**
Fécero. **AN.** (*warmly clasping Phormio's hand.*)
O mi Phórmio,
Válē! **PH.** Vale, Antiphó! bene, ita me dí ament, factum
gaúdeo. (*exeunt Antipho and Geta into Demipho's
house.*)

SC. 7.

PHORMIO.

Tantám fortunam de ímproviso esse hís datam!
Summa éludendi occásio est mihi núnc senes,   885

Et Phaédriae curam ádimere argentáriam,
Ne quoíquam suorum aequálium suppléx siet.
Nam idem hóc argentum, ita út datum est, ingrátiis 5
Ei dátum erit: hoc qui cógam, re ipsa répperi.
Nunc géstus mihi voltúsque est capiundús novos. 890
Sed hínc concedam in ángiportum hoc próxumum,
Inde hísce ostendam me, úbi erunt egressí foras.
Quo me ádsimularam ire ád mercatum, nón eo. (*exit with
a knowing wink at the audience.*) 10

ACTVS V.

SC. 1 [8].

DEMIPHO. CHREMES. PHORMIO.

(*Demipho and Chremes come out of the house of the former.
They advance to the front of the stage, so that Phormio at
his entrance crosses behind them.*)

DE. Dis mágnas merito grátias habeo átque ago,
Quando évenere haec nóbis, frater, próspere. 895
CH. Estne íta uti dixi líberalis? **DE.** Óppido. 12
Quantúm potest. nunc cónveniundus Phórmio est,
Priũs quám dilapidat nóstras trigintá minas,
Vt aúferamus. **PH.** (*Phormio had entered during Demipho's
last speech, and now, pretending to be unaware of his
presence, knocks loudly at the door and calls out to
the slave within.*) Démiphonem sí domi est 5

Visam, út quod—DE. (*tapping Phormio on the shoulder.*)
At nos ád te ibamus, Phórmio. 900
PH. De eadem hác fortasse caúsa? DE. Ita hercle. PH.
Crédidi:
Quid ád me ibatis? rídiculum: verēbámini
Ne nón id facerem quód recepissém semel?
(*pompously.*) Heus! quánta quanta haec méa paupertas ést,
tamen 10
Adhúc curavi unum hóc quidem, ut mi essét fides. 905
Idque ádeo venio núntiatum, Démipho,
Parátum me esse: ubi vóltis, uxorém date.
Nam omnís posthabui míhi res, ita uti pár fuit, 15
Postquám tanto opere id vós velle animadvórteram.
DE. (*hesitating and confused.*) At híc dehortatus ést me, ne
illam tíbi darem: 910
'Nam quí erit rumor,' ínquit, 'id si féceris?
Olím quom honeste pótuit, tum non ést data:
Eam núnc extrudi túrpe est': ferme eadem ómnia 20
Quae túte dudum córam me incusáveras.
PH. (*indignantly.*) Satís superbe inlúditis me. DE. Quí?
PH. Rogas? 915
Quia ne álteram quidem íllam potero dúcere:
Nam quó redibo ore ád eam quam contémpserim?
CH. (*nudging Demipho and prompting him, apart.*) 'Tum
autem Ántiphonem vídeo ab sese amíttere 25
Invítum eam,' inque. DE. Tum aútem video fílium
Invítum sane múlierem ab se amíttere. 920
(*authoritatively.*) Sed tránsi sodes ád forum, atque illúd
mihi
Argéntum rursum iúbē rescribi, Phórmio.
PH. Quodne égo discripsi pórro illis quibŭs débui? 30
DE. Quid ígitur fiet? PH. (*drawing himself up and speaking*

with great affectation of dignity.) Sí vis mi uxorém
dare,
Quam déspondisti. dúcam: sin est út velis 925
Manére illam apŭd te, dós (*pointing to himself.*) hic maneat,
Démipho.
Nam nón est aequom mé propter vos décipi,
Quom ego vóstri honoris caúsa repudium álterae 35
Remíserim, quae dótis tantundém dabat.
DE. (*bursting out into an open passion.*) I hinc ín malam rem
    cum ístac magnificéntia, 930
Fugitíve! etiam nunc crédis te ignorárier
Aut túa facta adeo? PH. Inrítor. DE. Tune hanc dú-
    ceres,
Si tíbi daretur? PH. Fác periclum. DE. Vt fílius 40
Cum illa hábitet apŭd te, hoc vóstrum consiliúm fuit.
PH. (*indignantly.*) Quaesó quid narras? DE. Quín tu mi
    argentúm cedo. 935
PH. Ímmo véro uxorem tú cedo. DE. (*seizing him.*) In
    ius ámbula.
PH. (*in a threatening tone.*) Enímvéro si porro ésse odiosi
    pérgitis—
DE. Quid fácies? PH. Egone? (*pointedly addressing
    Chremes.*) vós me indotatís modo 45
Patrócinari fórtasse arbitrámini:
Etiám dotatis sóleo. CH. (*with pretended indifference.*) Quid
    íd nostrá? PH. (*ironically.*) Nihil. 940
(*speaking in a loud voice.*) Hic quándam noram, quoíus
    vir uxorem—CH. (*in great alarm.*) Hém! DE.
    Quid est?
PH. Lemni hábuit aliam—CH. (*in abject despair.*) Núllus
    sum. PH. ex qua fíliam
Suscépit: et eam clam éducat. CH. Sepúltŭs sum. 50

PH. Haec ádeo ego illi iám denarrabo. **CH.** (*in a tone of piteous entreaty.*) Óbsecro,
Ne fácias. **PH.** (*with ironical surprise.*) Oh! tune ís eras?
DE. (*savagely.*) Vt ludós facit. 945
CH. Missúm te facimus. **PH.** Fábulae! **CH.** Quid vís tibi?
Argéntum quod habes cóndonamus te. **PH.** Aúdio.
(*with insolent bluster.*) Quid vós, malum! ergo mé sic ludi-
   ficámini 55
Inépti vostra púerili senténtia?
Noló, volo: volo, nólo rursum: cápe, cedo: 950
Quod díctum, indictum est: quód modo erat ratum, ín-
   ritum est. (*turns contemptuously on his heel.*)
CH. (*apart.*) Quo pácto aut unde haec híc rescivit? **DE.**
   (*apart.*) Néscio,
Nisi, mé dixisse némini, certó scio. · 60
CH. (*apart.*) Monstri, íta me dí ament, símile. **PH.** (*aside.*
   rubbing his hands with glee.) Inieci scrúpulum.
DE. (*apart.*) Hem!
Hicíne ut a nobis hóc tantum argenti aúferat 955
Tam apérte inridens? émori hercle sátius est.
Animó virili praésentique ut sís, para.
Vidés tuom peccátum esse elatúm foras, 65
Neque iam íd celare pósse te uxorém tuam:
Nunc quód ipsa ex aliis aúditura sít, Chreme, 960
Id nósmet indicáre placabílius est.
Tum hunc ínpuratum póterimus nostró modo
Vlcísci. **PH.** (*aside.*) Attat! nísi mi prospicio, haéreo. 70
Hi gládiatorio ánimo ad me adfectánt viam.
CH. (*apprehensively.*) At véreor ut placári possit. **DE.** (*laying*
   his hand on Chremes' shoulder.) Bóno animo es: 965
Ego rédigam vos in grátiam, hoc fretús, Chreme,
Quom e médio excessit únde haec susceptá est tibi.

PH. (*having overheard the preceding conversation.*) Itane
  ágitis mecum? sátis astute adgrédimini.   75
Non hércle ex re istius me ínstigasti, Démipho.
Ain tu? úbi quae lubitum fúerit peregre féceris,   970
Neque huíus sis veritus féminae primáriae,
Quin nóvŏ modo ēï fáceres contuméliam,
Veniás nunc precibus laútum peccatúm tuom?   80
Hisce égo íllam dictis íta tibi incensám dabo,
Vt né restinguas, lácrumis si extilláveris.   975
DE. (*stamping with rage.*) Malúm! quod isti dí deaeque
  omnés duint.
Tantáne adfectum quémquam esse hominem audácia!
Non hóc publicitus scélus hinc asportárier   85
In sólas terras! CH. (*tremulously.*) Ín ïd redactus súm loci,
Vt quíd agam cum illo nésciam prorsum. DE. (*vehemently*,
  trying to seize hold of Phormio.) Égo scio: 980
In iús eamus. PH. Ín ius? (*moving towards the door of
  Chremes' house.*) huc, si quíd lubet.
DE. (*hastening towards his own house.*) Adséquere, retine,
  dŭm ego huc servos évoco.
CH. (*in great fear, not venturing to touch Phormio alone.*)
  Enim néqueo solus: ádcurre. (*Demipho seizes
  hold of Phormio and tries to drag him back.*) PH.
  (*struggling.*) Vna iniúria est   90
Tecúm. CH. (*seizing Phormio by his other arm.*) Lege
  agito ergo. PH. Áltera est tecúm, Chreme.
(*A violent struggle ensues; the two old men not being strong
  enough to drag Phormio away, and Phormio being unable
  to gain the door of Chremes' house.*)
DE. Rape húnc. PH. Sic agitis? énĭmvero vocé est opus: 985
(*shouting.*) Nausístrata! exi. CH. Os ópprime. DE. (*trying in vain to put his hand over Phormio's mouth.*)
  Inpurúm vide,

Quantúm valet. **PH.** Nausístrata! inquam. **CH.** Non taces?
PH. Taceám? **DE.** Nisi sequitur, púgnos in ventrem íngere. 95
PH. Vel óculum exculpe: (*Nausistrata opens the door of Chremes' house.*) est úbi vos ulciscár probe.
(*As Nausistrata appears, Phormio throws off Demipho and Chremes to the right and left, and stands in the middle of the stage pointing towards her. Both the old men are panting from their exertions, and Chremes covers, with his back turned, at the extreme corner of the stage.*)

SC. 2 [9].

NAVSISTRATA. CHREMES. PHORMIO. DEMIPHO.

(*Nausistrata, having heard her name loudly called, comes out to see who is treating her so disrespectfully. Chremes tries to avoid his wife's eye.*)
NA. Qui nóminat me—? (*seeing that something extraordinary has happened.*) Hem! quid ístuc turbae est, óbsecro, 990
Mi vír? **PH.** (*sarcastically.*) Ehem! quid nunc óbstipuisti?
NA. Quís hic homo est? (*she pauses for the reply which Chremes does not give.*)
Non míhi respondes? **PH.** Hícine ut tibi respóndeat,
Qui hercle úbi sit nescit? **CH.** (*nearly beside himself with fear.*) Cáve ísti quicquam créduas.
PH. Abí, tánge: si non tótus friget, me énica. 5
CH. Nil ést. **NA.** Quid ergo? quíd ístic narrat? **PH.** Iám scies: 995
Auscúlta. **CH.** Pergin crédere? **NA.** Quid ego óbsecro

Huic crédam, qui nil díxit? PH. Delirát miser
Timóre. NA. Non pol témere est, quod tu tám times.
CH. (*trembling all over.*) Egŏn tímeo? PH. (*ironically.*)
    Recte sáne: quando nĭl times,   10
Et hŏc nĭl est quod ego díco, tu narrá. DE. Scelus! 1000
Tibi nárret? PH. (*with great contempt.*) Ohe tu! fáctum
    est abs te sédulo
Pro frátre. NA. Mi vir! nón mihi dices? CH. (*stammer-
    ing.*) Át— NA. (*mocking his stammer.*) Quid
    'at'?
CH. Non ópus est dicto. PH. Tíbi quidem: at scito huíc
    opu'st.
In Lémno—CH. (*crying out with alarm.*) Hem! quid aïs?
    DE. (*to Phormio.*) Nón taces? PH. clam te—
    CH. (*helplessly retreating to a corner.*) Eí mihi!   15
PH. uxórem duxit. NA. (*with a scream.*) Mĭ́ homo! di
    meliús duint.   1005
PH. Sic fáctum est. NA. (*covering her face with her hands.*)
    Perii mísera! PH. Et inde fíliam
Suscépit iam unam, dúm tu dormis. CH. (*to Demipho, in
    abject terror.*) Quíd agimus?
NA. (*indignantly.*) Pro di ínmortales! fácinus miserandum
    ét malum.
PH. Hoc áctum est. NA. An quicquam hódie est factum
    indígnius?   20
Démipho! te appéllo; (*turning her back on Chremes with
    disgust.*) nam cum hoc ípso distaedét loqui: 1011
Haécine erant itiónes crebrae et mánsiones diútinae
Lémni? haecine erat éa quae nostros mínuit fructus víli-
    tas?
DE. Égo, Nausistrata, ésse in hac re cúlpam meritum nón
    nego: 25

Séd ea quin sit ígnoscenda? **PH.** (*scornfully*.) Vérba fiunt
   mórtuo. 1015
DE. Nám neque neglegéntia tua néque odio id fecít tuo.
Éa mortem obiit : é medio abiit, quí fuit in re hac scrúpulus. 30
Quam ób rem te oro, ut ália facta túa sunt, aequo animo
   hóc feras. 1020
NA. (*passionately*.) Quíd ego aequo animo? cúpio misera
   in hác re iam defúngier.
Séd quid sperem? aetáte porro mínŭs peccaturúm putem?
Iám tum erat senéx, senectus sí verecundós facit.
Án mea forma atque aétas nunc magis éxpetenda est,
   Démipho? 35
Quíd mi hic adfers, quam ób rem expectem aut spérem
   porro nón fore? 1025
PH. (*coming forward and speaking to the audience like a
   town-crier*.) Éxequias Chreméti quibus est cómmodum ire, em! témpus est.
(*pointing triumphantly to Chremes*.) Síc dabo : age nunc,
   Phórmionem, quí volet, lacéssito :
Fáxo tali eúm mactatum, atque híc est, infortúnio. (*paces
   up and down the stage with insolent bravado.*)
(*changing his tone to one of contemptuous pity*.) Rédeat sane in
   grátiam : iam súpplici satis ést mihi. 40
Hábet haec ëi quód, dum vivat, úsque ad aurem oggán-
   niat. 1030
NA. (*with angry irony*.) Át meo merito, crédo : quid ego
   núnc commemorem, Démipho,
Síngulatim, quális ego in hunc fúerim? **DE.** Novi aeque
   ómnia
Técum. **NA.** Merito hoc meó videtur fáctum? **DE.** Minume géntium!
Vérum, quando iam áccusando fíeri infectum nón potest, 45

Ígnosce: orat, cónfitetur, púrgat: quid vis ámplius? 1035
PH. (*aside*.) Énimvero, priŭs quam haéc dat veniam, míhi prospiciam et Phaédriae.
(*approaching and addressing Nausistrata.*) Heús Nausistratá! priŭs quam huic respóndes temere, audí. NA. Quid est?
PH. Égo minas trigínta per falláciam ab illoc ábstuli:
Eás dedi tuo gnáto: is pro sua Pámphila emundá dedit. 50
CH. (*to Phormio, angrily.*) Hém! quid aïs? NA. (*with withering sarcasm.*) Adeón indignum hoc tíbi videtur, fílius 1040
Hómo adulescens si habet unam uxórem, tu senéx duas? Níl pudere? quo óre illum obiurgábis? respondé mihi.
(*Chremes shrinks away, utterly crushed.*)
DE. Fáciet ut volés. NA. Immo ut meam iám scias senténtiam,
Néque ego ignosco, néque promitto quícquam, neque respóndeo, 55
Priŭs quam gnatum vídero: eius iudício permitto ómnia. 1045
Quód ĭs iubebit fáciam. PH. Mulier sápiens es, Nausístrata.
NA. Sátĭn tibi est? CH. Satis? Ímmo vero púlchre discedo, ét probe —
(*apart to the audience.*) Ét praeter spem. NA. Tú tuom nomen díc: quid est? PH. Mihin? Phórmio:
Vóstrae familiae hércle amicus, ét tuo summus Phaédriae. 60
NA. Phórmio, at ego ecástor posthac tíbi, quod potero, quód voles 1050
Fáciamque et dicám. PH. Benigne dícis. NA. Pol meritúm est tuom.
PH. Vín primum hodie fácere quod ego gaúdeam, Nausístrata,

Ét quod tuo viro óculi doleant? **NA.** Cúpio. **PH.** Me
ad cenám voca.
NA. Pól vero voco. **DE.** Eámus intro hinc. **CH.** Fíat:
sed ubi est Phaédria, 65
Iúdex noster? **PH.** Iam híc faxo aderit. (*they all move
towards the door of Chremes' house, as the Cantor
comes forwards.*) **CANTOR.** Vós valete et plaú-
dite. (*curtain.*) 1055

METRA HVIVS FABVLAE HAEC SVNT

Ver. 1 ad 152 iambici senarii
„   153 trochaicus octonarius
„   154 et 155 trochaici septenarii
„   156 et 157 trochaici octonarii
„   158 et 159 trochaici septenarii
„   160 ad 162 iambici octonarii
„   163 iambicus quaternarius
„   164 ad 176 iambici octonarii
„   177 et 178 iambici septenarii
„   179 trochaicus octonarius
„   180 trochaicus septenarius
„   181, 182, 184 iambici octonarii
„   183 iambicus quaternarius
„   185 et 186 trochaici septenarii
„   187 et 188 trochaici octonarii
„   189 et 190 trochaici septenarii
„   191 trochaicus dimeter catalecticus
„   192, 193, 195 iambici octonarii
„   194 iambicus senarius
„   196 iambicus quaternarius
„   197 ad 215 trochaici septenarii
„   216 ad 230 iambici senarii
„   231 et 232 trochaici septenarii
„   233 ad 251 iambici octonarii
„   252 et 253 trochaici septenarii
„   254 ad 314 iambici senarii
„   315 ad 347 trochaici septenarii
„   348 ad 464 iambici senarii
„   465 ad 468 trochaici octonarii
„   469 et 470 trochaici septenarii
„   471 ad 478 iambici octonarii

Ver. 479 et 480 trochaici octonarii
„ 481 ad 484 trochaici septenarii
„ 485 clausula
„ 486 iambicus octonarius
„ 487 ad 489 trochaici septenarii
„ 490 iambicus senarius
„ 491 iambicus septenarius
„ 492 iambicus octonarius
„ 493 ad 501 trochaici septenarii
„ 502 et 503 iambici octonarii
„ 504 ad 566 trochaici septenarii
„ 567 ad 712 iambici senarii
„ 713 ad 727 iambici octonarii
„ 728, 730, 731 trochaici octonarii
„ 729 trochaicus dimeter catalecticus
„ 732 trochaicus septenarius
„ 733 et 734 iambici octonarii
„ 735 ad 738 trochaici octonarii
„ 739 ad 741 trochaici septenarii
„ 742 ad 747 iambici octonarii
„ 748 ad 764 iambici septenarii
„ 765 iambicus octonarius
„ 766 ad 794 iambici septenarii
„ 795 ad 819 iambici octonarii
„ 820 ad 827 iambici septenarii
„ 828 ad 840 iambici octonarii
„ 841 ad 883 trochaici septenarii
„ 884 ad 1010 iambici senarii
„ 1011 ad 1055 trochaici septenarii

NOTES.

Didascalia. The notices called διδασκαλίαι, concerning the origin and first performance of Plautine and Terentian comedies, were inserted after the titles in the MSS., probably by grammarians of the Augustan age.

Phormio. The reason of the title is given Prol. 26-8.

Ludi Romani or **Ludi Circenses** were celebrated in honour of Jupiter, Juno, and Minerva (Cic. Verr. 2. 5. 14), September 4th-19th. At first irregular, and lasting but one day, they became annual, Mommsen thinks, about 367 B.C., and extended to fifteen days by 44 B.C., a sixteenth being added in honour of J. Caesar after his death. The entertainments included a procession, chariot-races, displays of horsemanship, boxers, dancers, comedies, etc.

Aedilibus Curulibus. These magistrates had official superintendence of the public games, and often spent vast sums upon them to gain popularity with a view to their canvass for the consulship.

egere, 'brought out.'

L. Ambivius Turpio was the manager who produced all Terence's plays See p. 15. Cicero de Senect. 14. 48 mentions him as a good actor. With him is associated in all the *Didascaliae*, except that of the Hecyra, L. Atilius of Praeneste, of whom nothing further is known.

modos fecit ... tota. 'The music by Flaccus, slave of Claudius, on treble and bass flutes throughout.' According to Servius *tibiae inpares = tibiae Phrygiae*, i.e. two of unequal size and stops: *tibiae pares = tibiae Sarranae*, i.e. two of equal size and stops. *Tibiae* are also called *dextrae* and *sinistrae*. Probably *t. dextrae* were treble, *t. sinistrae* bass, so that *t. inpares* would be one of each. The Heauton Timorumenos was '*primum tibiis inparibus, deinde duabus dextris*,' as opposed to '*tibiis inparibus tota,*' the change of the music corresponding to the merrier character which the play assumed. Donatus, however, says that *t. dextra* = bass, and *sinistra* = treble.

Claudi, sc. *Servos*, who composed the music for all Terence's plays.

Graeca, i.e. *Comoedia Palliata*, wherein the scene and characters are Greek, as opposed to a *Comoedia Togata*, in which they are Roman, or at any rate Italian. See Introduction, p. 15.

Apollodoru. This archaic form, representing the Greek gen. sing. in -ov, is retained in the *Didascaliae*; cf. *Adelphoe* = 'Ἀδελφοί. Apollodorus of Carystus in Euboea, a writer of New Comedy (see p. 13), also composed the original of the Hecyra. He is said to have written forty-seven comedies and gained the prize five times, but some confusion exists between him and another comic poet, Apollodorus of Gela.

Epidicazomenos (Mid. voice), i.e. 'one who claims a girl in marriage as next of kin.' Donatus says that the real title was Ἐπιδικαζομένη (Pass. voice), from the girl claimed, and that the Ἐπιδικαζόμενος was a different play; but this seems improbable, as we should naturally expect ἡ Ἐπιδικασθεῖσα, not ἐπιδικαζομένη. Cf. 125 note.

facta IIII, 'produced fourth in order,' i.e. of Terence's comedies; the abortive attempt to represent the Hecyra being apparently not reckoned. See p. 15.

Cos. or **Coss.**, the usual abbreviation for *Consulibus*. The date was 161 B.C. See p. 15.

Prologue.

It had been the custom of earlier dramatists to give a plot of the Play in the Prologue. As dramatic art developed this was felt to be unnecessary, and Terence only followed the example set by Plautus in the Trinummus (if the Prologue of that play be authentic), in making the various characters of the comedy unfold its story to the audience. It was, however, an innovation either to write no Prologue at all—as at the first representation of the Hecyra, and possibly of the Andria—or to make the Prologue a vehicle for answering personal criticisms and attacking critics. The Prologues of the six plays of Terence are all genuine, while the twelve extant Prologues of Plautus are all spurious, with the possible exception of that to the Trinummus.

1. **postquam**, as in Ad. 1, almost = *quoniam* (*quom iam*), the fact being that the ideas of sequence in time and of causality fade imperceptibly into each other.

poeta vetus, i.e. Luscius Lanuvinus, his jealous rival, to whom Terence refers in all his prologues, except that of the Hecyra—in Heaut. 22 with the epithet *malevolus*. Cf. p. 15.

poetam. Terence never introduces his own name, as Plautus sometimes does, but calls himself *poetam*, *hunc*, or *hominem*.

Note the alliteration, which however Terence does not use so freely as Plautus, except in his prologues; cf. 4, 8, 11, 14, 17, 18, 22, 23, 29. Jordan calculates that an alliteration occurs in about every nine lines of Plautus and twenty lines of Terence. Cf. 334.

2. **studio**, sc *scribendi*.

4. **dictitat**, note the frequentative, 'is always saying.'

antehac, always scanned as two syllables in Terence.

5. Translate, 'that the plays ... are poor in execution and commonplace in style.' *oratio* is the manner in which the plot (*argumentum*) is worked out. *scriptura* is either (a) ' the style of the composition '= *stilus*, here and Andr. 12; or (β) 'the work composed;' cf. Hec. Prol. 2. 13 *ne cum poeta scriptura evanesceret*; ib. 24; Ad. 1.
    levi, opposed to *gravi*, 'stately.'
6. adulescentulum, more correct than *adolescentulum*.
7. cervam fugere etc. depend on *adulescentulum videre*. In Terence *video* is often followed by an Inf. with Acc. expressed or understood; sometimes by a Participle. as is the rule with Augustan writers. Cf. 177. We know nothing of the passage here alluded to, but we gather that the style of Lanuvinus was somewhat sensational and melodramatic. Insane delusions have often been represented on the stage, notably in the Ajax of Sophocles.
9. intellegeret, more correct than *intelligeret*.
    quom, always so spelt in Plautus and Terence. Latin writers till the end of the republican period avoided *u* after *u* or *v*. The correct form in classical Latin is *cum*.
    stetit, 'succeeded;' *stare* was technically used of a play in this sense. This is one of the very few instances in which Terence retains the archaic long quantity of a final syllable. Cf. Ad. 25 *augeāt industriam*. Cf. p. 30.
10. Actoris, possibly Ambivius Turpio. Lanuvinus might have retorted that this was true of the Hecyra.
13. lacessisset = *lacessivisset*. Syncope is more common in Terence than in Augustan Latin. Cf. 198 note.
14. prōlogum, in spite of πρόλογος; cf. *platĕa* and πλατεῖα, *crĕpĭdam* and κρηπῖδα, *prōpinare* and προπίνειν.
16. in medio etc., 'is for open competition among all.' Cf. ἐν μέσῳ κεῖται. For the opposite *e medio* see 967, 1019.
17. artem musicam = Gr. μουσικήν, which includes all literary, scientific, and artistic pursuits, opposed to γυμναστική. Translate, 'who cultivate dramatic art.'
18. ab studio studuit. The juxtaposition of two words of the same root is common in Terence. This is merely a special form of *Assonance*, and is to be distinguished from *Agnominatio* or *Paronomasia*, which, strictly speaking, is a play upon words of similar sound but different sense, something akin to a pun, e.g. Andr. 218 *inceptio est amentium haud amantium*. Paronomasia is fairly common in Plautus, but rare in Terence. The term is sometimes extended to a play upon different meanings of the same word, such as is not uncommon in Cicero, e.g. *ius Verrinum*. Cf. Dem. de Cor. 13.

rēicere, contracted form of *rejicere;* cf. 717, Verg. E. 3. 96 *reice capellas,* Hor. Sat. 2. 3. 283 *surpite = surripite.* Tr. 'to reduce to beggary.'

19. hic. Cf. 1 note.

20. audisset bene, 'he would have been well spoken of;' *audire bene* or *male* is often used thus, e.g. 359. Cf. καλῶς or κακῶς ἀκούειν.

21. rellatum = *red-latum* by assimilation. Lucretius uses both *rellatus* and *rĕlatus;* cf. 86 *redducere,* 646. Translate, 'Let him consider that he has been paid back in his own coin.'

22. dicundi. This was the archaic spelling of the Gerund and Gerundive. At the period of Terence the forms in *-undus* and *-endus* were used side by side for verbs of the third or fourth conjugation, except that *-undus* is never admitted where the verb-stem ends in *u* or *v*. The older form was much affected by Sallust, and is frequently used by Augustan writers, especially in legal or political phrases, e.g. *iure dicundo, res repetundae,* being most common in verbs of the fourth conjugation, *ire* and its compounds always retaining the form in *-undus,* while *gerundus* and *ferundus* are usually found in Cicero, Caesar, and Livy. This form is seldom used, as here (and 50), for the Gerund.

23. quom, 'although.' In Plautus often, in Terence occasionally, *quom* causal or concessive is followed by the Indicative. Cicero regularly uses this construction after such verbs as *laudo, gaudeo, doleo, gratulor,* and, if the reading be correct, in Off. 1. 44. 157 *atque ut apum examina non fingendorum favorum causa congregantur, sed, cum congregabilia natura sunt, fingunt favos; sic homines . . .* Cf. 208, 967. In this case it is easily seen how the idea of coincidence in time passes into that of 'although.' Roby, § 733.

Some editors place a note of interrogation after *facit,* but there is a good sense without a question. 'I will now say no more about him, though he on his side does yet more offend.'

de se is inserted to answer to *de illo,* emphasising the unprovoked character of the attack. The sense here given to *de* is unusual.

24. novam, sc. new to the Roman stage.

25. Epidicazomenon. Cf. note on Didascalia.

26. Latini etc., 'its Latin title is Phormio.' Bentley's emendation was *Graece, Latine.*

27. primas partis qui aget, 'the leading character,' Gr. πρωταγωνιστής.

Phormio, from φορμός, a mat, indicating the grovelling character of a parasite.

partis. The Acc. plural of such nouns of the third declension as form the Gen. plural in *-ium* was generally written *-eis* or *-is*. But from an early period, as inscriptions prove, there was considerable variety of usage. In the last century of the Republic the tendency seems to have been to write *-es* in common words, *-is* in others.

28. **parasitus** (παρά-σῖτος), lit. 'a companion at table.' The term soon acquired an invidious meaning, ' a needy hanger-on,' such as were admitted to the houses of the wealthy on condition of making themselves useful and agreeable by telling stories or singing songs for the amusement of the guests.

res, ' the action of the play.'

29. **voluntas vostra**, ' your good will.'

30. **date operam**, 'give us your attention.' Cf. 62 note.

per silentium, ' in silence' or 'silently;' cf. *per ludum*, ' in sport,' *per vim*, ' forcibly,' *per tumultum*, ' uproariously,' etc.

32. **quom per tumultum** etc. ' When our troupe was driven off the stage with uproar ' (Gr. ἐξέπεσε), referring to the first attempt to produce the Hecyra (see p. 15). Ambivius Turpio says in his Prologue Hec 33-6

> *Quom primum eam agere coepi, pugilum gloria,*
> *Funambuli eodem accessit expectatio,*
> *Comitum conventus, strepitus, clamor mulierum*
> *Fecere ut ante tempus exirem foras.*

Appeals for good behaviour were very necessary in the case of the miscellaneous throng which composed the audience in a Roman theatre, as in the Poenulus of Plautus, where nurses are requested not to bring in babies, *' ne et ipsae sitiant, et pueri pereant fame ; neve esurientes hic quasi haedi obvagiant.'*

grex, ' the troupe;' *dux gregis*, ' the manager,' who was also the chief actor, in this case Turpio, and so called in v. 33 *actor*.

33. This line probably refers to the successful performances of the Heauton Timorumenos and Eunuchus, as the Hecyra was not accepted by the public till 160 B.C. the year after the performance of this play.

34. **aequanimitas**, ' your kind attention ; ' cf. Ad. 24.

ACT I. SCENE 1.

Davus is a character introduced merely to assist in the explanation of the plot to the audience, in Greek πρόσωπον προτατικόν. He appears, purse in hand, to repay a loan to Geta, the confidential slave of Demipho.

35. **summus**, ' intimate.'

popularis, ' fellow-countryman.' If Davus = Dacus, it is likely enough that Terence might have considered him a fellow-countryman of Geta, as both Daci and Getae were tribes living on the banks of the

Danube. At Rome slaves were often named thus after their nationality; e. g. Syrus. *Popularis* may, however, merely = 'fellow-slave,' according to the custom, not yet obselete, of slaves to identify themselves with their masters.

36–7. erat ei etc. 'I had a trifling balance of money on a little account for some time due to him.'

rĕlĭcŭom. This word is always of four syllables in Lucretius and the older writers. Lucretius scans *rēlĭcŭos*. Catullus, Tibullus, Vergil, and Horace, unwilling either to lengthen the first syllable or to unite the two last, avoid the word altogether. Later it is used as a trisyllable, e. g. by Juvenal, *rĕlĭquus*. Note the diminutives.

38. id ut conficerem, sc. *oravit*, curious Ellipsis. Translate, 'could I settle it?' In colloquial language the principal verb is often omitted. Cf. 65, 80, 142, 144, 198, etc.

39. erilem filium = *eri filium*, a common phrase in Terence. Cf. 128 note. Such words as *erus, umerus, umor* were never spelt with an *h* until after the Augustan period.

40. credo, parenthetical, as often in the comic writers.

41. quam inique comparatum est, 'what an unfair arrangement it is.'

ii, so A, no MS. reading *ei* or *i*, which is commonly printed in deference to Ritschl on Pl. Trin. 17 (Prolegomena, p. 98). Priscian says that *ii* was pronounced as *i*, and probably was sometimes so written.

43. unciatim, 'ounce by ounce.' The *uncia* = $\frac{1}{12}$ of the *as* or *libra*, which was originally a pound weight of copper. Adverbs in *-tim* were probably old Accusative cases.

demenso, 'rations,' 'short commons,' which were served out to slaves, an allowance proverbially scanty: sometimes called *diaria* (*dies*), as being the daily portion, e. g. Hor. Ep. 1. 14. 40. Cf. ἁρμαλιή, Hes. Op. 765.

44. genium, 'his own self,' (from root GEN- in *gigno*). 'The Romans believed that every man had a genius, though their notions on the subject seem very confused. According to the name it should be the attendant on a man's birth, as it was believed to be the inseparable companion of his life. It represented his spiritual identity, and the character of the genius was the character of the man.' Mr. Macleane's note on Hor. Ep. 1. 7. 94. Cf. Hor. Od. 3. 17. 14 *Cras genium mero Curabis*, ib. Ep. 2. 2. 187,

> *Scit genius, natale comes qui temperat astrum,*
> *Naturae deus humanae, mortalis in unum*
> *Quodque caput, vultu mutabilis, albus et ater.*

Ib. 2. 1. 144, Pers. 5. 151 *indulge genio*. Cf. 70 note.

NOTES. LINES 36-50.

compersit, 'has saved,' spelt *comparsit* in the Calliopian MSS.
45. illa, i.e. the bride.
46. partum, sub. *sit*, the Ellipse making the phrase more emphatic.
47. ferietur alio munere, 'will be hit again,' a colloquial phrase for losing money which has a parallel in English. Propertius 4. 5. 44 uses *ferit* in a similar sense. In Pl. Trin. 247 *ibi pendentem ferit*, there is a play upon the ordinary and the colloquial meanings.
48. natalis dies, i. e. at the ἀμφιδρόμια, or name-feast, an Attic festival, at which the child was carried round the hearth. Birthdays were scrupulously observed among the Romans also, as occasions for gifts and feasts. Note the proceleusmatic in the second foot; see Introduction on Metres, p. 26.
49. initiabunt, a word of doubtful meaning in this place.
 (1) 'at his initiation,' either to the family *sacra*, or to the Eleusinian or other mysteries.
 (2) 'at his weaning,' because according to Varro children were then initiated to the rites of the deities who presided over eating, drinking, and sleeping, *Edulia* (or *Edusa*), *Potica*, and *Cuba*.
Admission to the family *sacra* is on the whole more probable, because the ceremony at weaning was purely Roman and so not likely to be here alluded to. See pp. 16-7. Some editors place only a comma after *dies*, supposing that the 'initiation' took place on the birthday; but it is more forcible to understand it as a fourth occasion for fleecing Geta.
50. mittundi. Cf. 22 note.
causa, 'pretext.'

Act I. Scene 2.

Davus is interrupted by the appearance of Geta, who is coming out to look for him. In the conversation which ensues Geta lets the audience know the position of affairs; how impossible he had found it to control the two young men, Antipho and Phaedria, of whom he had been left in charge; how Phaedria had become enamoured of a music-girl whom he was unable to purchase from her master Dorio; how Antipho likewise had fallen a victim to the charms of a young lady named Phanium, whom he had first seen at her mother's funeral; how by Phormio's assistance a suit had been trumped up against Antipho, who was asserted to be the next-of-kin to Phanium; how, no defence being made, the marriage had been hastily concluded, with the result that all parties were now dreading the return of the young man's father Demipho.

51. rufus, 'red-haired.' Davus wore a red wig. *Rufus* in this sense was a cognomen of several families at Rome. The sentence is an *Aposiopesis*; cf. 110.

praesto est, 'he is here.' An old Nom. *praestus* is found in an inscription, but it is only used as an adverb elsewhere.

52. obviam conabar, sc. *ire*, ' I was going to look for you.'

em. In Plautus and Terence *em* seems to be used as another form of *en*, while *hem* is an interjection expressive of any strong emotion. The MSS, however, vary so much that often the reading cannot be certainly determined. Here A gives *em*, tr. 'take it, here it is;' all other MSS. *hem*, which is adopted in the text with a colon after *accipe*, because it is dramatically more forcible. *Em* is often followed by an *Accusative*, sometimes with *tibi* added. Cf. 210, 847, etc.

53. lectum est, ' it is of full weight,' lit. 'picked-out;' cf. Pl. Ps. 1149 *Accipe: hic sunt quinque argenti lectae numeratae minae*.

conveniet numerus. sc. *nummorum*, etc. 'You will find the amount of my debt in full:' an idiomatic use of the Fut. specially common in Horace, e.g. Od. 1. 6. 1, 1. 7. 1, etc.

54. amo te, 'I am much obliged to you.' Cf. 478. Similarly, *amabo* = ' if you please.'

55. adeo res redit, 'things are come to such a pass.' Cf. 317. Reflections on the depravity of the age are very frequent in the comic writers, e. g. Pl. Trin. 1028–53, Ad. 441 5, etc.

redit, probably contracted from *rediit*; cf. 153, 706, Munro on Lucr. 3. 1042.

57. tristis, ' out of spirits;' it often = ' out of temper ' or ' morose ' in Terence, e. g. Ad. 79.

58. istuc, neuter of *istic, istaec, istoc* or *istuc*, a form of *iste* strengthened by the demonstrative affix -*ce*, as in *hic, haec, hoc*, and *illic, illaec, illoc* or *illuc*; cf. 77 note, 290, etc.

59. modo ut = *dummodo*; cf. 773.

abi, ' go to,' a common expletive, sometimes used in a good sense, more often threatening or contemptuous. Cf. 994.

sis = *si vis*, usually joined in colloquial language with an Imperative. Cf. 103 *sodes*.

62. hanc operam tibi dico, 'I am all attention:' *operam dicare* is somewhat stronger than *operam dare*, cf. 30.

63. senis nostri = Demipho.

Chremem. Like some other Greek proper names this word

follows more than one form of inflexion in Terence: e. g. *Chremem*, *Chremi* (gen.) And. 368, *Chremes* or *Chreme* (voc.); also *Chremetem* And. 472, *Chremetis* ib. 247, *Chremeti* infra 1026.

64. nostin ? = *novistine ?* The final *-e* of *-ne* is often dropped when affixed to words ending in *-ti*, *-is*, *-us*, *-a*, and the last syllable is then shortened. Cf. 194, 256, 275, etc.

quid ni? 'of course,' a conversational phrase.

quid? 'well;' used to introduce a new point in a narration or argument; frequent in this sense in Cicero. Cf. 147.

Phaedriam, sub. *nostin?*

65. tam quam te = *tam bene eum novi quam te.*

66. illi, i. e. Chremes; nostro, i. e. Demipho.

Lemnum. Lemnos became a dependency of Athens in the first Persian war and so continued until the Macedonian supremacy, a special clause in the peace of Antalcidas allowing Athens to keep Lemnos, Imbros, and Scyros.

Ciliciam. After the conquest of Alexander the Great, Greek civilisation spread to Cilicia, and Tarsus became a well-known school of philosophy.

67. antiquom, 'of old standing,' not old in years, which would have been *senem*, or *veterem*.

68. modo non, 'little short of.'

70. sic est ingenium, 'that is his way:' *ingenium* = the natural bent of his character or 'genius.' Cf. 44 note.

regem me esse oportuit, ''Tis *I* ought to have been the Croesus,' implying, I would have made a better use of my money than that. *Rex* was technically used for a wealthy powerful patron in relation to his clients and dependants: cf. 338, Hor. Ep. 1. 17. 20, Juv. 1. 36, etc.

71. hic (so A) with *relinquont ;* other MSS. read *hinc* with *abeuntes.*

72. provinciam etc., 'you undertook a hard commission.' Cf. Pl. Tr. 190.

73. mi usus venit, 'so I found it,' lit. 'experience came for me;' a familiar idiom, cf. Heaut. 553, 556, 557.

74. memini, 'I am sure that;' the word literally means 'to have in mind.'

deo irato meo, 'because my god was angry with me.' Every person had some special deity, under whose protection he supposed himself to be; a sort of divine 'patronus.' Cf. Pl. Poen. 2. 4 *dis meis iratissumis ;* Verg. A. 2. 396 *haud numine nostro.* We might render, 'I am sure that the charge was a freak of my evil genius.'

76. scapulas perdidi, 'I made my shoulders come to grief,' i.e. I got beaten for my pains.

77. **venere in mentem mi istaec;** *istaec* can be Nom. fem. pl. or Nom. neut. pl. (cf. 58 note); if taken here as fem. the sense is, 'I thought of those shoulders of yours;' if as neut. 'I thought of what you just mentioned.' The former seems preferable.

78. **advorsum stimulum calces,** sc. *iactare*, 'it is folly to kick against the pricks;' πρὸς κέντρα μὴ λάκτιζε. is a Greek proverb found in Aeschylus, Pindar, and Euripides, e. g. Aesch. Ag. 1624, Eur. Bacc. 795, Acts of the Apos. 26. 14.

The text of 77–8 is according to the best MS. authority.

Some editors give the whole passage to Geta (73–79), reading '*nam quae* (= *quaenam*) *inscitia est, Advorsum stimulum calces!*' as a quotation.

eis, 'for them,' dat. commodi.

79. **obsequi quae vellent,** 'to humour them in whatever they wished:' *quae*, a kind of Cognate Acc., cf. Ad. 990.

scisti uti foro, 'you know how to work the market :' *scisti = scivisti*. Note the close connexion between the Present and the full Perfect; 'you have understood' = 'you know.' Cf. 103.

80. **nil quicquam,** an emphatic pleonasm, common in colloquial language. Cf. 89, 630. There is an ellipse of *fecit*; cf. 440 note.

81. **puellulam.** Note the contemptuous diminutive.

82. **perdite,** 'to distraction;' *miser* is similarly used Ad. 522, etc.

83. **inpurissimo,** an abusive epithet, common in Terence.

84. **neque ... quicquam,** sc. *erat*, ' and there was not a penny to give,' sc. for her purchase.

85. **oculos pascere,** cf. Verg. A. 1. 464 *animum pictura pascit inani*.

86. **sectari.** Note the frequentative, 'dance attendance on her.' The word was used of the young men who frequented the society of the famous philosophers and sophists.

in ludum ducere, 'to escort her to her school,' i. e. where she had music lessons, her value as a slave depending on her accomplishments.

redducere. The double *d* is confirmed by Lucretius, who lengthens the first syllable, and it appears as a correction in D and Andr. 559 in **A**.

88. **exadvorsum ilico,** 'right opposite;' *ilico* (*in loco*) is occasionally used in early Latin in its original sense of *place*, not as later of *time*. Cf. Ad. 156 *nunciam ilico hic consiste;* infra 195.

89. *tonstrina*, in most MSS. *tostrina*, cf. *Cos. = Cons.*, note on Didascalia. Barbers' shops in classical, as in more recent times, were favourite resorts where the news of the day was learnt and discussed.

fere plerumque, pleonastic, cf. 80.

90. **dum iret,** Subjunctive of expected action, a form of Final Subj. Roby, § 692.

91. illi = *illic*, an archaic form often found in Plautus, sometimes in Terence, and perhaps in Vergil G. 1. 54, 251, 3. 17. Cf. 572, 772.

92. mirarier, historic Inf., a marked characteristic of Terence's style, wherein he is followed by Sallust. The archaic termination of the Inf. Pass. or Deponent in *-ier* is not unfrequent in Terence, but only when the antepenultimate is long. Cf. 206, 305, 306, 589, 603, 632, 640, 697, 931.

93. modo, 'just now;' cf. 221. With the following vivid narrative may be compared the corresponding scene in the Andria 105 sqq.

94. visum, is attracted into the gender of the Complement *onus*.

95. hic viciniae, 'hard by;' *viciniae* is most probably a Genitive (partitive) depending on *hic*; cf. Andr. 70 *huc viciniae*, and such phrases as *adhuc locorum* Pl. Capt. 382, *istuc aetatis* Heaut. 110; it might, however, be a locative.

97. ea sita est exadvorsum, 'the corpse was laid out opposite the door,' as was the custom. *sita* is more commonly used of a corpse when buried.

99. miseritum est, sub. *me*, 'I was moved with pity.'

101. commorat = *commoverat*.

102. voltisne eamus. *Volo* may be followed by the simple Inf., Acc. and Inf., Subj. with or without *ut*, or Acc. with a Part. Pass. Cf. 432.

visere. The Inf. of Purpose is used by Terence after *ire*, *mittere*, and *dare*, as well as *ut* with Subj. or Supine in *-um*: very rare in Augustan writers, and only in poetry, cf. Verg. A. 1. 527 *non ferro Libycos populare Penates venimus*, Hor. Od. 1. 2. 7 *pecus egit altos Viscre montes*.

103. sodes = *si audes*, 'if you please.' Cf. 59 *sis*.

vēnimus, Perf. tense, 'we arrive.' Note the vigour of the *Asyndeton*.

104. et quo magis diceres, 'and all the more reason for saying so is that . . .'

106. horrida, 'unkempt.' This scene is closely imitated by Molière, Les Fourberies de Scapin, Acte I, Sc. 2.

107. vis boni, 'the very essence of beauty.' Cf. δύναμις τοῦ καλοῦ.

108. inesset . . . extinguerent. The use of the Imperf. Subj. for the Pluperf. Subj., for the sake of greater vividness, is an idiom often found in the best authors; sometimes even a Pres. Subj. is substituted. Cf. Madvig, Lat. Gr. § 347, obs. 1–3; infra 119, 297, 299, 468, etc.

110. satis scita est, 'she is pretty enough.' Cf. Andr. 486 *perscitus puer*, 'a very fine boy;' the more usual meaning being 'witty,' 'clever,' 'sensible,' e. g. 820.

For the *Aposiopesis* cf. 51.

111. **scin quam** = *scisne quantum*. Cf. Cic. Phil. 2. 41 *vide quam te amarit.*

quo evadat vide, 'see the sequel.'

112. **anum, i. e.** Sophrona.

recta, sc. *via,* 'straight.'

113. **enim.** Terence often uses *enim* or *nam* as a particle of emphasis; cf. 332, 338, 487, 555, 694, etc. In 983 *enim* in this sense begins a sentence; cf. Ad. 168, Pl. Trin. 1134. Vergil and others constantly employ the same idiom, and there is a similar use of γάρ in Greek, especially in ἀλλὰ γάρ = *sed enim.* Cf. 615 note.

se negat, sc. *id facturam esse.* Such an ellipse is common enough in colloquial language, e. g. 383, 447, 519, etc.; cf. 38, 440 notes.

117. **nescire,** Historic Inf., cf. 92; like the Historic Pres. it can be followed either by a primary or historic Subjunctive in dependent sentences.

119. **non** = *nonne*, as regularly in Terence and Plautus. Indeed it is doubtful whether *nonne* was found in the original MSS. of these writers, *-ne* or *non* being used indifferently. However all existing MSS. read *nonne* 768, Andr. 238, 239, Ad. 660. Cf 260, 392, 525, 856. *Non* is sometimes thus used in *spoken* language by later writers, e. g. Cic. Cat. 1, Liv. 4. 4, etc.

veniam daret, 'would he not have given him permission;' for the tense cf. 108 note.

120. **indotatam.** The dowry was the first point looked to by a father who was arranging a match for his son.

122. **quid fiat?** The Subj. depends on *rogas* or some similar word understood. It is common in the indignant or excited repetition of a question asked by another; e. g. 382, 685.

123. **homo confidens,** 'an impudent rascal.' *Confidens* usually in a bad sense, but cf. Andr. 855. Note *homō* here, *homŏ* 411.

qui, an old form of the ablative or locative, used by Plautus and Terence in several senses :—

(1) as a relative, referring to any gender and either number. Cf. 655, 770, 889.

(2) as a final particle, with the Subjunctive—'in order that.' Cf. Ad. 950.

(3) as an interrogative adverb, in direct or indirect questions,— 'how,' 'why?' Cf. 130, 330, 381, 396, 398, 799, 855, 915. In this sense it is common in Horace, Cicero, etc.

(4) as an indefinite particle with words of emphasis—'somehow,'

NOTES. LINES 111–137.

Gr. πώς, e. g. *hercle qui, edepol qui, quippe qui, numqui*, etc. Cf. Ad. 800.

(5) introducing curses, πῶς, *ut*, 'would that,' 'O that.' Cf. the present passage, Pl. Trin. 923, 997.

perduint, archaic form of *perdant* (as *duint* for *dent*), used often by Plautus, thrice by Terence, twice by Cicero. Plautus also employs *perduim, perduis, perduit*. In Terence occur *duim, duit, duint*, in Plautus *duim, duis* or *duas, duit, duint*. Cf. 519, 713, 976, 1005.

125. **proxumi**. In older Latin superlatives were spelt *-umus* not *-imus*. Julius Caesar is said to have introduced *-imus*. By a law of Solon if a citizen died leaving his estate to a daughter in default of male issue, provided no special arrangement had been made in the father's will, her next of kin (ἀγχιστεύς) was bound to marry her, or to provide an additional dowry. Cf. Diod. Sic. 12. 18. 2, 3. Such a girl was called ἐπίκληρος, and the person making application for her hand was said ἐπιδικάζεσθαι. Cf. note on Didascalia; Numbers xxxvi. 8. Demosthenes in Mac. 1067 *ad fin*. tells us that there was a fine of 500 drachmae for a πεντακοσιομέδιμνος, 300 for a ἱππεύς, and 150 for a ζευγίτης.

127. **scribam dīcam** = γράψομαι δίκην. Cf. 329, 439, 668. Here there is a play upon *dīcam* and *dĭcam*.

128. **paternum amicum** = *patris amicum*; cf. 39 note.

me, sub. *esse*.

130. **qui**, 'how;' cf. 123 note.

131. **quod ... commodum**, 'as shall be good and expedient for my case.' Most editors connect this clause with what follows, but it seems more natural to take it with *confingam, quod* being adverbial.

132. **quom ... refelles**. The case was to be undefended.

133. **mihi paratae lites**, 'I am in for a row;' a colloquial usage, cf. 219, Ad. 792.

quid mea, sc. *refert?* 'What care I?' Cf. 389, 723 notes.

134. **iocularem audaciam!** Acc. of exclamation. 'What amusing impudence!'

135. **vincimur**, plural because Geta identifies himself with Antipho.

137. **quid te futurum est?** 'What will become of you?' Cf. 811. *Facere, fieri, esse*, in the sense of 'to do anything with a person,' or 'become of a person,' are constructed with the Instrumental Ablative without a preposition, rarely with *de* and the Ablative. Cf. Andr. 614 *quid me faciam?* infra 426, Pl. Trin. 405 *quid factum est eo?* Ad. 996 *sed de fratre quid fiet?* Cic. Fam. 14. 4. 3 *quid Tulliola mea fiet?* When a Dat. is found in similar phrases it is a *Dat. commodi vel incommodi*, e. g. Andr. 143 *quid facias illi qui*, etc., 'what would you do to the man who,' etc. Cf. Hor. Sat. 1. 1. 63.

138. Pyrrhus in Ennius An. 204 is made to say . . . *quidve ferat fors virtute experiamur*. This makes the sentiment in Geta's mouth yet more absurd.

placet, ' well said,' ' hear, hear.'

139. hem! Cf. 52 note.

140. laudo, ' bravo!'

ad precatorem adeam, credo, ' I am to betake myself to an intercessor, I suppose.' From allusions in the comedians, e.g. Heaut. 976, 1002, we gather that it was customary for a slave when in trouble to enlist the services of a *precator*. For *credo* parenthetical cf. 40.

141. amitte hunc, ' let him off;' often in this sense in Plautus and Terence. Donatus says, *quod nos dicimus dimittere, antiqui etiam dicebant amittere*. Cf. 175, 176, 414, 918.

142-3. si quicquam, sub. *faciat*.

nil = an emphatic *non* ; so also *nullus*, cf. Andr. 370 *CH. Liberatus sum hodie, Dave, tua opera. DA. Ac nullus quidem.*

tantummodo non addit, 'the only thing he leaves out.'

vel ōccidito, ' you may kill him if you like.' In such sentences reference is made to the original sense of *vel* (from *volo*). On the quantity see p. 28. The Future Imperative is often used in familiar language of a single act, for the sake of greater emphasis. Cf. 166, 984.

144. paedagogus ille. Phaedria is comically so called because he escorted his music-girl to and from her school like a παιδαγωγός.

qui citharistriam, sc. sectatur. Cf. 86.

145. quid rei gerit? 'how does he get on?'

sic, tenuiter, 'so so, but poorly.' Cf. 5.

146. Note the Hiatus after *fortasse*, at a change of speaker. See p. 31.

147. quid? 'I say.' Cf. 64 note.

148. quoad expectatis? 'when are you expecting?' lit. ' up to what point of time are you waiting for?' *quoad = quod ad = ad quod.*

150. portitores, 'the custom-house officers,' who collected the *portoria*, harbour-dues. All letters brought by sea seem to have passed beneath their censorship. Cf. Pl. Trin. 793, 810.

151. num quid aliud me vis? 'is there anything further you want me for?' A common formula of leave-taking. Cf. 458, Ad. 247, Pl. Trin. 192, Hor. Sat. 1. 9. 6. Note the double Acc. after *vis*, as after a verb of asking. This construction is used by Terence more freely than by Augustan writers, e.g. with *incuso* 914, *condono* 947.

ut bene sit tibi, the polite rejoinder, which was changed by Dempa in reply to Syrus, Ad. 432. to ' *Mentem vobis meliorem dari.*'

152. hoc, i.e. the money paid to him by Davus.
Dorcio. Dorcium was probably Geta's wife. Female names often ended in *-ium*, an endearing diminutive, e.g. Phanium, Glycerium. A slave's marriage was not recognised at law either at Athens or Rome. Strictly the woman was in Latin a *contubernalis*, though practically she is sometimes termed *uxor*, e.g. Ad. 973.

Act I. Scene 3.

The young men, Antipho and Phaedria, appear in conversation. The former is dreading his father's return, the latter reproaches his cousin for his faint-heartedness, and contrasts his own love-lorn condition with that of Antipho, who is in full possession of the object of his affections.

153. adeon rem redisse, 'to think that things have come to such a pass.' Terence often uses the Acc. and Inf. to express excited or indignant exclamations and questions, as also Cicero, Livy, etc.

-ne is frequently found in such forms, because a question is implied if not expressed, e.g. 339; but naturally *-ne* is not used if the clause begins with *non*, e.g. 232-3.

redisse. For the spelling see 55 note, 460, etc.

qui mihi consultum optume velit esse, 'though he is anxious for my best interests,' a common phrase, *consultum esse* being used impersonally. *qui* is here concessive.

154. ut, repeated from line above. The clause *patrem ut extimescam* should be taken before *qui mihi* etc.

ubi in mentem eius adventi venit, 'when a thought of his arrival occurs to me.' This construction of *venire in mentem* with a Genitive is not unfrequent in Cicero, e.g. Sull. 6. 19 *cum matronarum ac virginum veniebat in mentem*. The phrase is almost equivalent to *meminisse* in meaning and so takes the same construction. It may be impersonal as here, or personal with the subject thought of in the nominative, as Liv. 8. 5 *non venit in mentem pugna apud Regillum lacum*. Cf. Madv. § 291, obs. 3. All MSS. give *venit*, except that the late corrector of A has introduced an *A*, whence most editors read *veniat*.

adventi, archaic for *adventûs*. In Old Latin the Gen. of U-Stems ended in *-uos*. In Terence a form in *-uis* once occurs, Heaut. 287 *anuis*, but the Gen. in *-i*, as though from an O-Stem, is common. Only the form *-ûs* is employed by Augustan writers, but Ennius, Lucretius, Plautus, and Terence use both forms side by side. We find in Terence *adventi, domi, fructi, ornati, quaesti, tumulti*. Neither Plautus nor Terence ever write *domûs*.

155. **quod**, 'whereas,' both here and 157 *quod* is an adverbial Acc. loosely used as a connective particle, a characteristic idiom of comic diction.

ut par fuit, 'as was right;' *par* is so used by Cicero.

156. **quid istuc?** 'what do you mean by that?' The MSS. give *quid istuc est? est* is omitted, following Bentley, *metri causa*.

qui, causal, 'seeing that you.' Cf. 471.

157. **quod.** Cf. 155 note, Cic. Fam. 14. 4. 1 *quod utinam minus vitae cupidi fuissemus;* and for *id* following *quod* Andr. 258 *quod si ego rescissem id prius*, etc.

utinam ne. Cicero uses both *ne* and *non* after *utinam*.

158. **neu** is for *et ne*, as *neque* is for *et non*.

neu cupidum eo inpulisset, 'and had not urged on my desires to that act:' *eo* lit. 'thither,' i.e. to the marriage. Cf. 201.

159. **non potitus essem**, 'I should not have won her.'

fuisset . . . dies, 'then I should have been wretched for the next few days.'

160. **cotidiana.** Neither the spelling nor the quantities of this word seem to have been settled. Martial, 11. 1. 2 writes *cŏtīdiana* or *quŏtī- diana*, Catullus 68. 141 (139) *cōtīdĭana* or *cōttĭdĭana*, though R. Ellis and most modern editors of Catullus replace the word by some con- jectural emendation.

audio, 'I understand.'

161. **dum expecto** etc. Antipho continues his sentence, not heeding Phaedria's *audio*.

consuetudinem, 'loving intercourse,' often so used in Plautus and Terence.

162. The order is '*Aliis aegre est quia quod amant desit: tibi dolet quia (quod amas) superest*. Tr. ' others fret from lack of bliss: you from surfeit.' For *dolet* impersonal cf. Ad. 272.

164. **quidem hercle certo.** Phaedria tries to make his sentence as emphatic as possible by the repetition of intensive words. Cf. Andr 347 *mea quidem hercle certe in dubio vita est*, Gr. τοιγάρτοι, τοιγαροῦν.

165. **ita me di bene ament**, 'heaven preserve me.' Cf. 883, 954.

166. **iam depecisci morte cupio**, 'now would I gladly close the bargain with my life:' *morte* is Abl. of price, cf. Pl. Bacch. 865 *pacisci cum illo paulula pecunia potes*.

tu conicito cetera, 'do you now compare the other points:' *conicere* = to place two propositions side by side, and so to draw a conclusion from them; cf. Gr. συμβάλλειν, and Juv. 6. 436 *committit vates et comparat*.

168. **ut ne addam**, 'not to mention.' Terence uses *ut ne = ne* negative purpose, e. g. 245, 314, 415, Andr. 259, and also *= ut non* negative result, e.g. 975. So Cicero, e.g. Verr. 2. 4. 28 *nam res celatum voluerat . . . ut ne multi illud ante perciperent oculis quam populus Romanus:* see a curious instance in Rosc. Amer. c. 20, where *ut ne =* 'provided that not :' ib. Lael. 42, 43, 60, 65. etc.

ingenuam liberalem, 'a lady born and bred.'

171. **scelere**, 'rascal.'

quo = *quocum*, which the later MSS. give.

172. **plerique omnes**, 'almost all of us;' the same phrase is found Andr. 55, Pl. Trin. 29.

nostri nosmet poenitet, 'we are ever discontented with our lot.'

nosmet. The suffix *-met =* 'self' is attached to *ego* and *tu*, rarely to *meus*. Conversely *-pte =* 'self,' 'own,' is commonly affixed to possessive pronouns, rarely to personal pronouns; while *-te* is found with cases of *tu* only. Cf. 280, 467, 766, 914.

173. **videre**. Plautus and Terence usually prefer the form in *-re* of second pers. sing. pass. to that in *-ris* except for metrical reasons. Cicero and Vergil follow the same custom except in the Pres. Ind. On the other hand Livy and Tacitus seldom use the form in *-re*.

174. **de integro**, 'freely.' The phrase Andr. 26 = 'anew.' In both cases the derivative meaning (*in* privative and stem of *tango*) is easily traced.

etiam (Gr. ἔτι), 'even yet,' as often.

175. **retinere, amare, amittere.** So all MSS. Most editors, seeing the alternatives *neque mittendi nec retinendi* in 176, get rid of *amare*; e.g. *retinere amorem an mittere* (Dz., Fleck., etc.): *retinere eam anne amittere* (B. and W. following Dz. first ed.). Bentley reads *retinere amare an mittere*. To add *amare* to *retinere* is no doubt more loverlike than logical, but that seems hardly sufficient reason for altering Antipho's words, which all MSS. give without variation.

For *amittere* cf. 141 note.

176. **ut neque mihi sit amittendi.** So A with Donatus and Servius. This reading involves the scansion *mihī*, which is uncommon in Terence. B C D E G P with A_2 insert *eius* after *sit*. If this reading be accepted it is an instance of the gerund used in a purely substantival sense, with a genitive after it, 'of the dismissal of her;' cf. Heaut. 29 *novarum qui spectandi faciunt copiam*, Hec. 372 *eius* (sc. *uxoris*) *videndi cupidus recta consequor*. This construction, which also occurs in Plautus, Lucretius, Cicero, and Suetonius, is instructive as

showing how entirely the gerund was recognised as a verbal noun. One MS. F gives *mi ius sit*.

177. **videon ... advenire?** 'Do I see Geta come running hither?'
178. **ipsus** = *ipse*, common in Plautus and Terence.
ei, interjection, often written *hei*.

ACT I. SCENE 4.

Geta appears in great perturbation, having heard of the sudden arrival of Demipho. Phaedria and the slave try to screw Antipho's courage to the sticking-point, but in vain. When the old man is seen approaching Antipho hurriedly decamps, leaving his cousin to bear the brunt of his father's anger.

179. **nullus es**, 'you are done for,' a colloquial phrase. Cf. 942, Andr. 599.

celere. This is the usual form of the adverb in Terence.

reperis. Here *repperis* is found in A B C D F P, *reppereris* in D_2 G and Priscian, *repereris* E. Probably *reperis* is the true reading, as mistakes of this sort often occur in the MSS.; e. g. in 192 five good MSS. read *repperiam* for *reperiam*.

180. **te inpendent**. A very rare construction, *inpendere* being followed by Dat. or *in* with Acc. Cf. Lucilius *ut quae res me inpendet agatur*, also Lucr. 1. 326 *mare quae inpendent*. Lucretius also uses *incidere* and *accidere* with an Accus.

181. **uti**, 'how,' as often.

183. **quidnam?** 'about what?' adverbial Acc.

184. 'Then I have but a moment to consider this affair.'
punctum temporis is rather a favourite phrase of Cicero. Cf. στιγμὴ χρόνου.

185. **quod**, sc. Antipho's marriage.

186. **laterem lavem**, 'I should be washing a brick;' a translation of the Greek proverb πλίνθον πλύνεις. The meaning is, 'it would be worse than useless.' Greek bricks were made of clay baked in the sun, so that the more they were washed the more dirty they would become. Cf. Xen. Hell. 5. 2. 5.

187. **quom ... tum**. This sentence shows well how these conjunctions, at first purely temporal, come to be used as particles of connexion. Here you might translate, 'while'... 'then,' or 'not only' .. 'but also.'

animi is a Locative like *humi, domi*, etc.: cf. Ad. 610 *discrucior animi*.

188. **nam absque eo esset,** 'for were it not for him.' Plautus and Terence only use *absque* in the protasis of conditional sentences with *si* omitted as here. In the Augustan period *absque* is only used in a few quasi-juridical formulae, e. g. *absque sententia*, 'without judgment.' Cf. Pl. Trin. 832, 1127.

absque was formed by adding *-que* (its copulative force being lost) to *abs*, which was a collateral form of *ab* (cf. ἐκ, ἐξ), used before words beginning with *c, q, t*. As early however as Plautus, *abs* is rarely found except before *te*. Cicero usually wrote *abs te* up to about B. C. 55. Occasional uses of *abs* in later authors. e. g. Livy, are probably intentional archaisms. In *as-pello, as-porto, a-spernor* (for *as-spernor*), the *b* has fallen out. Cf. Pl. Pers. 159 *abs chorago*; infra 201, 378, 617, 840.

189. **vidissem** = *providissem*, colloquial.

190. **aliquid convasassem,** 'I should have packed a few things together:' *convasare* is ἅπαξ λεγόμενον in classical literature. It is taken from the military phrase *vasa colligere*, 'to pack up.' The few things would be of course his master's property.

protinam, archaic form of *protinus*, but scanned *prŏtĭnam*, ἅπαξ λεγ. in Terence. All MSS. here read *protinus*, but Donatus gives *protinam*, which is required by the metre and confirmed by Pl. Bacc. 374.

192. **qua quaerere insistam via?** 'where lit. by what road' shall I begin to look for him?' *insistere*, 'to stand' or 'press upon' may be constructed with a Dat. or *in* with Abl. or a simple Acc.; while in the sense of 'to set about,' 'to begin,' it is followed by an Inf. as here. A confusion of these usages probably accounts for the reading *viam* in A F G. In Eun. 294 *quam insistam viam*? there is no Infinitive.

193. **nescio quod magnum ... malum,** 'some great calamity or other.' If *nescio quod* had meant 'I do not know what,' the following verb would have been in the Subj. *Nescio quid*, 'somewhat,' is often used to qualify a verb or adjective. *Nescio* may be scanned as a dactyl, or as a spondee by Synizesis. Cf. p. 31.

194. **sanun** = *sanusne*.

ibi plurimum est, 'he is mostly there.'

195. **ilico** may here be of place, 'where you are,' or of time, 'at once.' Cf. 88 note.

satis pro inperio, sub. *loqueris*, 'you give your orders peremptorily enough.'

196. The grammatical order is *Ipse est obviam, quem volui*, 'here is the very man I want.' Cf. Andr. 532 *eccum ipsum obviam*.

197. **cĕdŏ,** 'tell me.' This archaic imperative ('tell me' or 'give

126   *PHORMIO.*

me') is used by Cicero. The plural *cette* is only found in old Latin. Cf. 321, 329, 398, 550, 642, 692, etc.

    verbo expedi, ' explain it in a word.'

    198. **meumne** = *meumne patrem vidisti?* a striking ellipsis.

    intellexti. A similar syncope (*is* being omitted) of verbs whose Perf. Ind. ends in *-si, -xi*, is used by Latin poets:

    (1) in the second pers. sing. Perf. Ind. (often), e.g. *dixti* (often), e.g. 537, and second pers. plur. (rarely).

    (2) in Perf. Infin. Cf. Ad. 561 *produxe*, Heaut. 32 *decesse*, ib. 1001 *iusse*.

    (3) in all persons sing. and first pers. plur. of Pluperf. Subj.; but none of this set occur in Terence.

The syncope of *-avisti, -avissem, -ovisti, -ovissem*, etc., into *-asti, -assem, -osti, -ossem,* etc., is too common to require detailed notice.

    Hem! This is an exclamation of surprise at Antipho's consternation. Phaedria, not having so guilty a conscience, had not been so quick to catch Geta's meaning.

    199. **quid ais?** a common phrase in Terence; used,

    (1) as a request for information, usually when a remark has not been heard or understood, as here. Cf. 833.

    (2) as an exclamation of surprise or anger at some remark which seems scarcely credible, e.g. 755, 873, 1040.

    (3) to introduce a new point in conversation, or to call attention, like *dis donc.* 'What do you say to this?' 'look here.' Cf. 798 note.

    200. **nam** etc. may follow on from *quid agam?* or *nam quod* may = *quodnam*, as is not unfrequent in Terence, e.g. 732.

    201. **eo.** Cf. 158. Both *eo* and *meae* are here scanned as monosyllables.

    abs. Cf. 188 note.

    Phānium was Antipho's young wife.

    203. **fortis fortuna adiuvat,** 'fortune favours the brave,' a proverb found in most languages. Cf. Menan. Fr. τόλμῃ δικαίᾳ καὶ Θεὸς συλλαμβάνει, Soph. Fr. 12 (Brunck), οὐ τοῖς ἀθύμοις ἡ τυχὴ συλλαμβάνει, Verg. A. 10. 285 *audentes fortuna iuvat.*

    204. **non sum apud me,** 'I am not myself at all;' a colloquial phrase, cf. Andr. 408, 937.

    nunc quom maxume, 'now most particularly.' Cf. Ad. 518, Andr. 823.

    ut sis, sc. *apud te.*

    206. **inmutarier,** 'change my nature,' lit. 'change myself.' Many cases occur where traces of the old Middle Voice can be clearly seen under Passive forms. Cf. 92 note.

    208. **quom hoc non possum,** 'since I cannot do this.' Cf. 23 note.

hoc nil est: ilicet, 'this is nonsense: let us be off.'
ilicet = *ire licet* was a formula of dismissal from an assembly, funeral, or other ceremonial gathering; see Conington's note on Verg. A. 6. 231. Cf. Ad. 791, where *ilicet* = 'it is all up.'

209. quin abeo? 'why do I not go?' equivalent in meaning to 'I am off.' Note the following uses of *quin* (*quí-ne*):

(1) 'why not?' either in direct or indirect questions. As may be seen from the present passage this meaning passes easily into 'indeed,' 'verily,' without a question. Cf. 429, 538, 1015.

(2) with Imperatives. This use is a natural development of the first; for *quin taces?* is equivalent in sense to *tace*. Cf. 223, 350, 486, 857, 882, 935.

(3) as a corroborative particle, 'indeed,' 'verily;' sometimes further strengthened by *etiam*. Cf. Ad. 262 *quin omnia sibi post putavit esse prae meo commodo*.

(4) in the common sense, 'but that,' after verbs expressing doubt, prevention, or the like, with a negative. Cf. 272, 697, etc.

210. quid si adsimulo? 'what if I assume an air.'
em! Cf. 52 note. In 212 *em istuc* scans as *ĕm ĭstuc*.

212. par pari ut respondeas, 'take care to answer tit for tat:' *ut* is here used elliptically, like ὅπως (Goodwin's Moods and Tenses, § 45, note 7), depending on some Imperative like *cave* or *fac* understood.

213. saevidicis is ἅπαξ λεγόμενον.
protelet, only ante- and post-classical, probably derived from *pro* and *tendo*, and so not connected with either Gr. τῆλε or *telum* (*tex-lum*), 'a missile weapon.' *Protelum* is used by Cato and Lucilius for 'a team of oxen harnessed in single file,' thence in Lucr. 2. 531 *undique protelo plagarum continuato*, 'a continuous succession of blows,' ib. 4. 190. So too in legal language *protelare* = 'to prolong by successive delays.' Here it forcibly expresses the idea of a rapid succession of attacks which might prevent Antipho from getting in a word of defence. Tr., 'lest in his anger he should rout you with his furious broadsides.'

214. coactum to esse, sub. *responde*.
tenes? 'do you understand?' In the same sense in Andr. 300, 349, 498, etc.

215. in ultima platea, 'at the bottom of the street.' For *platĕa* cf. 14 note.

219. litis. Cf. 133.

220. ego plectar pendens, 'I shall be hung up and flogged.' Cf. Pl. Trin. 247 *ibi pendentem ferit*.

221. modo. Cf. 93 note.

223. aufer mi 'oportet.' ought me no oughts.' Phaedria means 'stop your platitudes and tell me something practical.'

quin. Cf. 209 note.

225. ad defendendam noxiam, ' to protect ourselves from blame.' Cf. 266.

226. ' That Phormio's suit was righteous, all plain sailing, sure to win, most equitable.'

vincibilem may be either Active ' convincing,' or Passive 'easy to be maintained.' In Augustan Latin verbal adjectives in *-bilis* have nearly always a passive signification; but in earlier periods the meaning is often active. Cf. 961 and Ad. 608 *placabilius;* Verg. G. 1. 93 *Boreae penetrabile frigus* ; Ov. Met. 13. 857 *penetrabile fulmen ;* Hor. Od. 1. 3. 22 *dissociabilis* (*Oceanus*) ; *exitiabilis* = *exitialis* in Plautus, Cicero, Livy, Ovid, and Tacitus; Lucretius uses *genitabilis, mactabilis ;* Horace has *illacrimabilem Plutonem* (act.), and *illacrimabiles urgentur* (pass.), Munro Lucr. 1. 11, Livy 31. 17, and 9. 26 *exsecrabile*.

227. em! ' see now ! '

230. subcenturiatus, ' as a reserve,' lit. 'a man to fill a vacancy in a *centuria*.' Geta is fond of military metaphors. Cf. 320, 346–7.

In this Play, as in the Adelphi, the division of Acts and Scenes in the MSS. is dramatically impossible, and is doubtless due to a copyist's ignorance. This edition adopts the arrangement found in practice to be the most natural and convenient, but the old numbering of Acts and Scenes is preserved in brackets for purposes of reference.

In MSS.	In this edition
Act I ends at line 230.	Act I ends at line 314.
,, II ,, 464.	,, II ,, 566.
,, III ,, 566.	,, III ,, 765.
,, IV ,, 727.	,, IV ,, 893.

Terence probably wrote his plays to be performed without a break. The division into Acts was most likely made by grammarians of the Augustan or a later age.

ACT I. SCENE 5. [ACT II. SCENE 1.]

Demipho is boiling over with rage at his son's unauthorised and imprudent marriage. Phaedria loyally defends his cousin, and assisted by Geta makes every possible excuse. Between them they manage to divert the old man's wrath upon Phormio's head.

231. itane tandem, etc., ' is it possible that A. has actually married a wife?' *itane* emphasises the question which is further strengthened by *tandem*, as frequently in Cicero. Cf. 315, 373, 413, 527.

232. **ac mitto inperium,** 'and not to mention authority.' Cf. 293. The Calliopian MSS. give *age* for *ac*.

233. **revereri.** Cf. 153 note. The subject *eum* is omitted, as often in Terence before an Infinitive.

234. **monitor.** Cf. Hor. A. P. 163 *iuvenis monitoribus asper*. In law, 'a prompter for counsel.'

vix tandem! sc. *meministi mei*, or some such words; spoken ironically. Cf. Andr. 470 *vix tandem sensi stolidus*.

235. **aliud cura,** 'think of something else,' 'try again.'

237. **causam tradere** etc., i. e. as a *praevaricator*. Tr. 'but the deliberate betrayal of the case without a word!'

238. **illud durum,** 'that's a poser.'

242. **meditari,** 'to rehearse.' Cf. 248.

advorsam aerumnam, 'the attacks of trouble.'

243. **peregre** is used for 'coming from abroad,' 'going abroad,' and 'rest abroad.' Cf. 970.

cogitet, sub. *quisque*.

245. **communia esse haec,** 'let him think that these are common misfortunes.'

ut ne quid. Cf. 168 note.

The text gives the MSS. reading. Many editors follow Cicero's version as quoted Tusc. 3. 14. 30:

Pericla, damna, peregre redicns semper secum cogitet
. . . .
Communia esse haec, nequid horum umquam accidat animo novum.

246. **deputare esse in lucro,** 'to reckon as clear gain;' *deputare* depends on *oportet*, supplied from 242.

248. **meditata,** one of the many instances of a deponent Perf. Part. used in a passive sense: cp. 242 note.

249. **A** reads *molendum esse*, which cannot stand with *habendae compedes*. B C E F P and Donatus give *usque*.

The *pistrinum* answered to our 'tread-mill' as a means of punishment.

250. **opus ruri faciundum.** To degrade a confidential body-servant to be a farm-labourer would be of course a severe punishment.

opus often means farm-labour in Terence, e. g. 363.

251. Cf. the similar parody of Demea's words by Syrus, Ad. 425-9.

255. **salvom venire,** sc. *gaudeo*. The ordinary salutation to one who has arrived after a journey. Cf. 286.

credo, 'I take that for granted.' Cf. 610.

258. **confecistis,** 'you have trumped up.'

259. **id,** Cognate Acc. 'about that:' so *quod* in 263, 1052. *O! ar-* seems to scan as one syllable: cf. 360, 368, 853, 930, Introd. p. 31.

I

260. **egon...suscenseam?** 'Could I help being angry with him?' Cf. 297, 304 notes.

262. **lenem patrem illum . . . me,** 'that I, formerly (*illum*) the kindest of fathers.'

264. **similia omnia,** 'it's all of a piece.' **congruont.** Cf. 9 note.

266-7. 'When A gets into trouble, B is his advocate: when B is in a scrape, A turns up: it's a co-operative concern.' Cf. 835-6.

hic as Nom. Sing. is usually short in Plautus and Terence, long in Augustan poets. See however 1028.

268. **inprudens,** 'unwittingly,' because he knows nothing of Phaedria's love-affairs.

269. **cum illo haud stares,** 'you would not be his partisan:' *stare ab aliquo* or *ab alicuius causa* = ' to be on a man's side:' *stare pro aliquo* = ' to be a man's champion.'

270. **si est,** ' if it is the fact.'

271. **minus ... temperans,** 'he was inconsiderate as to fortune or to fame,' i.e. in marrying a penniless girl of ignoble birth. *rei* and *famae* are probably Genitives: *temperare* in this sense usually takes a Dat., but *temperans* is also found with a Gen. = ' temperate in.'

272. **quin** follows the idea of ' prevention ' contained in *non causam dico.* Cf. 209 note.

276-7. **adimunt diviti... addunt pauperi.** This would have been more likely at Athens than at Rome.

280. **tua iusta,** ' the rights of your case.'
tute. Cf. 172 note.

281-2. **functus adulescentuli est Officium liberalis,** 'he acted like an ingenuous youth.' *Fungor* governs the Acc. in Plautus and Terence, except in Ad. 603 *tuo officio fueras functus,* where the MSS. give the Abl. Conversely *fruor* is constructed with the Abl. in Terence, except in Heaut. 401, where the Acc. is found: *utor* takes an Abl. except perhaps in Ad. 815, but *abutor* an Acc. For *potior* cf. 469 note. Lucretius constructs *fungor, fruor, potior* with Acc.; *abutor* with Acc. and Abl.

284. **timidum.** Antipho being really of a timid nature, cf. 204 sqq., this statement sounded plausible enough.

obstupēfecit. When preceded by a short syllable the *e* in compounds of this class is usually shortened, following the analogy of the ' Iambic Law,' p. 27, but Catullus 64. 361 has *tepĕfaciet.*

289. **iam dudum . . . audio,** ' I have been hearing you for some time;' cf. Fr. *depuis longtemps je vous entends.*

dudum may refer to time past, immediate or distant; e.g. 537, 786, 838 'just now,' in Pl. Trin. *quam dudum?* = ' how long ago?' Cf. 459, 471.

290. horunc = *horum-ce*, cf. 58 note.

292. servom hominem, 'one who is a slave;' both *homo* and *mulier* are often thus used in apposition. At Athens the evidence of slaves was only taken under torture, at Rome not at all against their masters, except in certain specified cases.

293. dictio. Verbal substantives in *-io* are sometimes followed by the same case as the verb: e.g. Andr. 44 *exprobratio est inmemori*. Still more remarkable is the use of the Acc. by Plautus after *receptio*, *curatio*, *tactio* (very often after the last).

mitto. Cf. 232.

294. do is Fleckeisen's emendation for *addo* or *adde*. It gives a better sense and seems necessary for the metre.

297. dotem daretis. Cf. 125 note, and for the tense 108 note. Cf. Verg. A. 4. 678 *eadem me ad fata vocasses*, 'you should have invited me to share your fate,' where the context makes it almost = *debebas vocare*; ib. 8. 643 *at tu dictis, Albane, maneres,* = *debuisti manere*; Cic. pro Sulla 8. 25 *ac si, judices, ceteris patriciis me et vos peregrinos videri oporteret, a Torquate tamen hoc vitium sileretur*; infra 298, 468, Heaut. 201-2 *fortasse aliquantum iniquior erat . . . pateretur*, i.e. 'he should have borne it.' These Subjunctives are 'Jussive,' expressing an unfulfilled obligation in past time. Roby 670.

298. qua ratione, 'on what account.' There is a play on the word *ratio* which Demipho uses as 'reason,' Geta as 'a money account.' Cf. Pl. Trin. 418-9:—

LE. *Aequaquam argenti ratio comparet tamen.*

ST. *Ratio quidem hercle adparet: argentum* οἴχεται.

299. dēerat. In this verb *ce* is scanned by Synizesis as *ē* by Vergil, Catullus, etc., as well as by Terence.

sumeret, sc. *mutuom argentum*, 'he should have borrowed it.'

302. crederet, 'would have given us credit.' At Rome the *Lex quina vicenaria* (*Lex Plaetoria*) forbade loans to young men under five and twenty; cf. Pl. Ps. 303; as did also the *Senatus-consultum Macedonianum*. But it is not clear that we have here a specific allusion to Roman law, which is against our author's custom; cf. p. 16.

303. potest, impersonal, as often in Terence: e.g. 402, 640, 674, 818.

304. egon . . . ut patiar. Note the emphatic *ego*. Madvig (§ 353 obs.) explains this construction as = *fierine potest ut* etc. Cf. 669, 874, 955, etc. Sometimes *-ne* is omitted, e.g. Andr. 618; sometimes *ut*, e.g. supra 260. Translate, 'to think that I should put up with her marriage with him for a single day.'

305. **nil suave meritum est,** 'they have deserved no indulgence,' lit. 'nothing indulgent has been deserved' sc. 'by them.' The Perf. Part. Pass. of *mereo* is used by Cicero, Livy, etc., though not often. Donatus interprets *nihil mihi mercedis suave est ut ego illam cum illo nuptam feram,* 'nothing could persuade me to permit the marriage.'
commonstrarier. Cf. 92 note.

307. **nĕ(m)pe,** often scanned thus in Plautus and Terence, when the first syllable is unaccented. In some MSS. it is then written *nepe.* See Introduction on Prosody, p. 30.

308. **iam faxo hic aderit,** 'I will fetch him here at once.'
faxo. Plautus and Terence use the following: *faxo* (Ind.), *faxim* (Subj.) *faxis, faxit* (Ind. or Subj.), *faxīmus* (Subj.), *faxitis* (Ind. or Subj.), *faxint* (Subj.). Cf. 554.

Three views are held with regard to these forms:—

(1) They may be syncopated forms for *fecero, fecerim,* etc.; cf. Zumpt. § 161, Peile Etymology, p. 197.

(2) They may be archaic futures, formed exactly like the Greek by adding -*so* to the verb-stem, e. g. *fac-so*=*faxo* as πραγ-σω=πράξω; the tense in -*sim* being the Subjunctive; cf. Roby, §§ 291-3, Madv. § 115 f.

(3) King and Cookson (p. 463) consider *faxo, faxim, amasso, amassim,* etc., to be conjunctive and optative forms of the sigmatic aorist. Cp. 742.

The philological uncertainty is not removed by the practical usage of these forms. In the present passage it is quite an open question (cf. 681 note), but *faxo* is often used where a Fut. simple would naturally stand, and in Ad. 847-8 is a direct co-ordinate of *faciam* Fut. The Subjunctive form is never used as a Perf. Subj., but always as a Fut.; cf. the epitaph of Ennius,

Nemo me lacrimis decoret nec funera fletu
Faxit. Cur? volito vivu' per ora virum ;

the common phrase *di faxint* expressive of a wish, Hor. Sat. 2. 3. 38 *cave faxis,* and the use of *ausim.* Vergil, Livy, Ovid, and Horace occasionally employ these forms, and *di faxint* is found even in Cicero. Cf. 742 note. As regards construction *faxo* is followed four times in Terence by the Fut. Ind., here, 1055, Eun. 285, 663, thrice by the Pres. Subj., Ad. 209, 847 (placed after the Subj.), and Andr. 854. It is also constructed with an Acc. and a Perf. Part. Pass., infra 1028. Probably the Indicative is grammatically independent: cf. 358 note. Augustan writers always use the Subjunctive construction.

foris, 'out,' an Abl. plur. of the obsolete *fora,* used as an adverb meaning 'rest out of doors:' so *foras* = 'motion out of doors.'

309. **adduc.** Terence always uses *duc* in the simple form, but in

composition either -*duce* or -*duc*. A always gives the shorter form if the metre does not require the longer, except in Heaut. 744 TRADVCEHVC: conversely the later MSS. always read the longer form except for metrical reasons, e. g. Eun. 377, and one MS. F which gives *traduc* in Heaut. 744. Of Imperatives usually syncopated Plautus sometimes writes *dice, duce*, never *fere*, and in both the comic poets *face* often appears, but only at the end of lines, e. g. 397, 674. Otherwise Terence uses the shortened forms. The rule in Augustan Latin was to use exclusively *dic, duc, fer, fac*, and similarly in the compounds of *duco, fero*, and those of *facio* which retain *a* in the stem; but other compounds of *facio* and those of *dico* retain the final *e* : e. g. *educ, affer, calefac*, but *confice, edice*.

311. The order is, *Ego devortar hinc domum salutatum deos penatis*.

313. **adsient**, archaic for *adsint*. Terence uses *siem, sies, siet, sient*: also *possiem, possiet, adsiet*. Cf. 446, 508, 514, 635, 675, 773, 806, 822.

314. **ut ne**. Cf. 168 note.

ACT II. SCENE 1 [2].

In the interval between the Acts Geta has met Phormio and informed him of the arrival and the anger of Demipho. Phormio is confident that he can carry the matter through; he boasts of the impunity with which he has preyed upon the wealthier citizens, and describes the delightful freedom from anxiety enjoyed by a parasite.

315. **itane . . . ais.** Tr. 'Do you really mean to say' etc. Cf. 231 note. The metre requires *patris* or *ais*.

admodum, 'certainly.' An affirmative answer may also be expressed by *etiam, ita, factum, oppido, sane, scilicet, sic, vero, verum*, etc.: or by repeating the verb, e. g. *hoc facies? faciam*: or by a pronoun, e. g. *hoc facies? ego vero*. Cf. 316, 382, 524, 811–12.

oppido, 'very much so,' a colloquial word, found in Cicero's Letters, etc., but not in his Orations; obsolete in the time of Quintilian. The derivation is doubtful. Festus says it arose from a frequent answer to an enquiry as to a man's crops, '*quantum vel oppido satis est.*' Whence *oppido* became equivalent to '*valde multum.*' Cf. 763, 896.

318. **tute hoc intristi**: tibi omne est exedendum, a proverb, lit. 'you have mixed the mess, you must eat it up.' In English, 'you have made your bed and you must lie upon it.' Cf. Auson. Id. vi *Tibi quod intristi exedendum est : sic vetus verbum iubet, | Compedes, quas ipse fecit, ipsus ut gestet faber.*

intristi=*intrivisti*, from the rare *intero*, referring here to the grating of various ingredients into a mortar, and then pounding them.

319. **eccere**, 'see there!' from *ecce* and *re* ('in fact') or *rem*.

320. quid si reddet? 'What if he shall give the girl back?' It might however be, 'What if he shall reply?' Cf. 877 note. Note that from 317 to 320 Phormio is buried in thought, uttering aloud only disconnected fragments of sentences, and paying no attention whatever to Geta's ejaculations.

321. cedo senem, 'bring the old fellow out.' Cf. 197 note.

322. crimine, 'reproach.'

323. derivem, 'divert,' a metaphor from turning the current of a stream (*de-rivus*).

325. in nervom erumpat, 'should end by landing you in the stocks.' Cf. 696.

nervom, lit. 'a sinew,' then 'a fetter,' especially used of a fetter for the feet and sometimes the neck, like our stocks or pillory. This use of *erumpat* is colloquial.

326. periclum, 'trial,' its original sense.

iam pedum visa est via, 'I can keep my feet out of harm's way by this time,' said with reference to *in nervom*.

327. usque ad necem, 'almost to death,' 'within an inch of their lives.' Notice this sense of *usque ad*, 'right up to, but just stopping short of.'

328. hospites, here 'aliens,' Gr. ξένοι.

quo magis novi, sc. *viam*, from 326, 'the better I know the way, the oftener I do it,' or, 'the better I know them,' etc.

329. cedo dum, 'tell me now.' *dum* is often used by the comic writers as an enclitic with Imperatives and Interjections, e.g. *ehodum*; and we also find *quidum* (interrogative) and *primumdum*. In later Latin this use of *-dum* is confined to *agedum*, *agitedum*, and *nondum*, *nedum*, *vixdum*, *dudum*, *interdum*. Cf. 594, 784, etc.

en umquam. These words are often used together (some write *enumquam*) in animated questions where the answer 'no' is expected: *en* serving to arrest attention. Cf. 348.

iniuriarum . . . dicam, Gr. αἰκίας δίκην, or in aggravated cases γραφὴν ὕβρεως. Tr. 'that a prosecution for assault was brought against me.' Cf. 983.

330. qui istuc? 'how is that?' Cf. 123 note.

tenditur, so all MSS. Most modern editors prefer *tennitur*, which is mentioned by Donatus as a various reading, probably representing the vulgar pronunciation.

Cf. Old English proverb, 'Stones and sticks are flung only at fruit-bearing trees.'

332. quia enim, 'because indeed.' Cf. 113 note.

illis . . . illis. Note the very uncommon use of the same pronoun to contrast two sets of people. On the stage the actor's gestures would prevent the possibility of mistake.

334. Notice the emphatic alliteration. Cf. 1 note. In default of payment of damages legally awarded, both Athenian and Roman law authorised the creditor to seize the person of the debtor (*addictus*) and treat him as a slave.

337. illo, sc. Antiphone.

338. immo enim. Cf. 113 note.

regi, 'his patron.' Cf. 70 note.

339. tene asymbolum venire, 'to think that you should come with no contribution to the feast.' It was a common Greek custom that each person dining should contribute his quota, called συμβολή in Greek, *collecta* by Cicero de Or. 2. 57. 233. Cf. Andr. 88 *symbolam dedit, cenavit.* Cf. 153 note. Hence the use of *immunis*, 'without a gift,' in Hor. Od. 4. 12. 22, Verg. G. 4. 244, Pl. Tr. 350.

340. otiosum ab animo, 'easy in mind:' *ab* denotes here, as often, the direction from which the matter in question is viewed. Cf. *a fronte, a tergo*, etc.

341. ringitur, 'he chafes,' lit. 'he snarls.'

tu rideas, 'you can laugh.'

342. prior bibas, etc., 'you can drink before him, you can have a better place at table.'

dubia, 'puzzling.' Cf. Fr. *embarras de richesse*, Hor. Sat. 2. 2. 77 *vides ut pallidus omnis Cena desurgat dubia.*

347. postillā=*posteā*, only ante-Augustan. Tr. 'directly after that you may play with him as you please.' Cf. 705.

ACT II. SCENE 2 [3].

Geta, pretending not to see the entrance of Demipho with his friends, defends his master with much simulated warmth; while Phormio affects righteous indignation. Demipho assails the parasite hotly, but meets his match. Phormio is not to be out-faced, but answers threat with threat; and though at one time nearly nonplussed by forgetting Stilpho's name, eventually leaves the field victorious.

348. en umquam. Cf. 329 note.

350. age. All Calliopian MSS. with A_2 read *ages*. The meaning would be the same. Cf. 209 note. Tr. 'now do you attend to this.'

351. ego hunc agitabo, 'I will stir him up.'

pro deum inmortalium, sub. *fidem:* cf. *pro divom fidem* etc. The interjection *pro* does not affect the case of the word before which it stands; cf. *pro Iuppiter!* Cf. 757 note, 1008.

356. After 355 is inserted in the MSS.,
PH. Nec Stilphonem ipsum scire qui fuerit? GE. Negat.
This must be a gloss, as is shown clearly by 386-9.

357. ignoratur, 'is disowned.' Cf. Pl. Trin. 264, Verg. A. 6. 615, 780

358. vide avaritia quid facit. Note the Indicative. 'In conversational or animated language a question is often put logically though not grammatically dependent on another verb or sentence, e. g. on such expletives as *dic mihi, loquere, cedo, responde, expedi, narra, vide: rogo, volo scire, fac sciam, viden, audin, scin,* etc. So frequently in Plautus and Terence, even where later writers would make the question dependent and use the Subjunctive. Compare, 'Tell me, where are you?' and 'Tell me where you are.' Roby § 751. Cf. 987.

359. Geta, as well as Phormio, is of course playing a part, intending to be overheard by Demipho.

male audies. Cf. 20 note.

360. Tr. 'What impudence! *he* is actually going to prosecute *me*.'

ultro, lit. 'beyond what might be expected;' contrasted with *sponte,* which merely means 'willingly.' Here Phormio does not wait to be made a defendant, but intends, as Demipho thinks, himself to prosecute. This meaning of *ultro* may be expressed here by emphasising the pronouns. Cf. 769. *O! au-* seems to scan as one syllable. Cf. 259.

362. illum, sc. Phanium's father, cf. 357.

norat = *noverat:* Indic. because the supposition was represented as a fact.

iam grandior, 'of some considerable age.' Notice this use of the Comparative; cf. Vergil's *iam senior* etc.

363. quoi in opere vita erat, 'who worked for his livelihood.'

365. interea, 'during that time.'

366. The order is, *narrabat hunc cognatum suom neglegere se.*

367. quem ego viderim etc. 'the most worthy man perhaps that I have seen in my life.' The Subjunctive probably qualifies what would otherwise be a downright statement, as is done in English by 'perhaps.'

368. videas te atque illum, ut narras, 'compare yourself and him according to your account,' i. e. 'what a contrast between such an excellent man as you describe and a rascal like yourself.' The meaning must be uncomplimentary to account for Phormio's rejoinder. Some explain thus, 'do *you* see to your stories about yourself and him, it is nothing to us;' or, 'see what lies you are telling about yourself and him.' Bentley's version, *vidisti nullum ut narras,* has the merit of simplicity. For scansion of *I in,* cf. 259, 360 notes.

i in malam crucem! 'go and be hanged.' Gr. ἔρρ' ἐς κόρακας. Cf. 930 *i hinc in malam rem*.

369. nam etc. This follows immediately on 367, Phormio disregarding Geta's interruption.

370. hanc, i. e. Phanium. Note the scansion ŏb hānc ĭnĭ | mĭcĭtĭ | ās etc. Cf. Introd. on Metres.

373. tandem. Cf. 231 note.

carcer, 'jail-bird.'

374. extortor ... contortor, 'you rascally robber, you pettifogging rogue.' *Contortor* is ἅπαξ λεγ., as is *extortor* in classical Latin.

378. adulescens, 'my young gentleman.'

abs te. Cf. 188 note.

bona venia, 'with your kind leave.'

379. potis est, 'it is possible:' *potis* may refer to a subject (rarely plural) of any gender, or may be used impersonally. The neuter *pote* is similarly employed, e. g. 535, but, unlike *potis*, is generally found without *est*. As a rule *potis* stands before vowels, *pote* before consonants. Neither *potis* nor *pote* occurs in Augustan prose.

380. tuom ... istum. The addition of *istum* emphasises *tuom*, and gives moreover a contemptuous turn to the phrase.

381. qui, 'how;' cf. 123 note.

diceret. The regular sequence of tenses would require *dixerit*. It is perhaps to be explained by the preceding *fuisse* which carries back the thought to past time, though grammatically the verb is of course dependent on *explana*.

382. nossem? Cf. 122 note.

383. ego me nego, sc. *nosse* (*novisse*).

tu, qui ais, 'do you, who make the assertion.'

384. enicas, 'you are worrying me to death.' Cf. 856.

386. perdidi, 'I have forgotten.'

387. subice, 'prompt me.'

388. temptatum, 'to try your tricks on me.' Supine in -*um*.

389. atque adeo. Note the uses of *adeo*—

1. 'so far,'
    (*a*) of space, 55.
    (*b*) of time, 589.
    (*c*) of circumstance, 497, 932.
2. as an intensive particle with
    (*a*) pronouns (common), 645, 906, 944.
    (*b*) adjectives or adverbs, 679. Heaut. 386.
    (*c*) conjunctions, as here. Tr. 'and after all'...
    (*d*) verbs, Andr. 759 *propera adeo puerum tollere*. Heaut. 170.

Vergil constantly uses it in this intensive sense, e. g. A. 3. 203 *tres adeo ... soles,* 'three whole days,' ib. 7. 629 etc.

3. 'Moreover,' 'besides' (rare).
quid mea, sc. *refert.* Cf. 133, 723 note.

392. **non te horum pudet?** The same meaning is expressed Ad. 754 by *non te haec pudent?* the verb being either personal or impersonal in Terence: but when personal the Nominative is usually a neuter pronoun. The above seems more probable than to refer *horum* to Demipho's friends.

393. **talentûm** = *talentorum*, as *nummûm* etc. An Attic talent = 60 minae = £243 15s. Cf. 644.

394-5. **esses proferens** = *proferres*. This is an early instance of the tendency of Latin, as of other languages, to become 'analytic;' i. e. to express changes of case, tense, mood, voice, or person by the addition of separate words, e. g. prepositions, auxiliary verbs, pronouns, etc., instead of by case-endings or verbal inflexions. The latter method is called 'synthetic.' Greek is a good example of a 'synthetic,' English of an 'analytic' language. Analytic varieties are, however, more frequent in Greek than Latin. Cf. And. 508, 775 *ut sis sciens* = *ut scias,* Cic. Verr. i. 40 *distributum habere* = *distribuisse:* infra 946, 974.

atavo, 'great-great-great-grandfather.' The ascending steps of paternal ancestry were *pater, avus, proavus, abavus* (= *avi-avus*), *atavus, tritavus* (= *avi-avi-avus*).

396. 'Exactly so: on coming before the court,' i. e. to claim his inheritance.

qui. Cf. 123 note.

397. **face,** archaic for *fac,* cf. 309 note.

398. **cedo.** Cf. 197 note. **qui.** Cf. 123 note.

eu, Gr. εὖ, so *euge,* Gr. εὖγε. Tr. 'well done our side.'

400. **si fuerat.** The Pluperf. Indic. after *si* is rare.

401. **filium narras mihi?** 'What! talk to me of my son?' Terence sometimes uses *narrare* = 'to speak about,' 'to mention.'

402. **potest,** impersonal, cf. 303.

403. **magistratus adi,** 'make an application before the magistrates,' so followed by *ut* and Subj. because equivalent to a verb of asking.

405. **solus regnas.** Cf. Ad. 175 *regnumne, Aeschine, tu hic possides?* Pl. Trin. 695 *quid? te dictatorem censes fore?* This can hardly be considered as a distinctively Roman allusion, since a 'tyrant' at Athens was almost as great a bug-bear as a 'king' at Rome. Phormio would of course lay special emphasis on *alterum, eadem, bis,* as well as on *solus regnas* and *soli.*

To have a case heard twice was illegal at Athens, cf. Dem. Lept.

NOTES. LINES 392–440.

p. 502; but at Rome there might be a '*restitutio in integrum*,' cf. 451.

409. ut . . . si instead of the usual *quasi*, because *ut* naturally follows *itidem*.

410. dotis dare etc. The logical order would be, *abduc hanc, minas quinque accipe, id dotis quod lex iubet dare*. The omission of the subject of *dare* makes the statement more general, as we should say in English, 'the dowry which the law orders one to give;' *dari* would have been more usual, *dare* being probably more colloquial. Demipho's excitement quite accounts for the irregular order of the clauses.

 abduc. Cf. 309 note.

 minas. The Attic mina = 100 drachmae = £4. 1s. 3d.

411. homŏ. Cf. *homō* 123.

413. tandem. Cf. 231 note.

414. amittere = *dimittere*. Cf. 141 note

415. ut ne. Cf. 168 note.

418. at nos unde, sc. *proxumi sumus?* 'but where does she get us from?'

419. 'actum,' aiunt, 'ne agas,' 'the proverb says, "don't kill a dead dog."' The Latin proverb is from the law-courts, 'don't bring on a case already decided,' cf. Ad. 232.

420. ineptis. Terence only uses the verb here and Ad. 934.

 sine modo, 'do you just let me alone:' *modo* emphasises the Imperative. Cf. 496.

426. tu te idem melius feceris, 'it would be better to do the same with yourself,' i. e. to leave the house yourself. It is best to consider *te* as Abl. after *feceris*, cf. 137 note, and *idem* as neuter.

427. advorsom is rarely, as here, put after its case; cf. Sall. Jug. 101. 8 *quos advorsum ierat*.

428. infelix, 'wretch.'

429. quin. Cf. 209.

432. te visum . . . velim? 'should I wish for the sight of you?' Cf. 102 note.

435. hoc age, 'attend to this:' a common phrase.

439. dicam tibi inpingam grandem, 'I will bring an action against you with swingeing damages.' Cf. 127 note.

440. si quid opus fuerit. The constructions of *opus* and *usus* are,

(1) *personal*, with the thing needed in the Nom. as a subject. The phrase may be completed by *ad* with an Acc., or by an Abl. which is sometimes a Perf. Pass. Part., e. g. 762 *quid facto opus est*, more rarely a supine. Cf. Roby, § 507, infra 563 note, 593.

(2) *impersonal*, with the thing needed in the Abl. which may be a substantive, adjective, or participle, very rarely in the Gen. (twice in Livy) or Acc. (twice in Plautus).

With either construction in place of an Abl. or a Nom. is sometimes found an Infinitive or Acc. and Infinitive, e. g. 560. The person who needs is in the Dative. Cf. 584, 666, 715–16, 1003.

domo me, sc. *arcesse*. Cf. 38 note.

ACT II. SCENE 3 [4].

Demipho consults his friends. They severally give opinions diametrically opposed to each other, leaving Demipho in greater uncertainty than before. The whole scene is pervaded by a delicate humour peculiarly Terentian.

442. **hisce**. The strengthening affix -*ce* is usually found with *hic* before words beginning with a vowel or *h*. The Nom. Fem. Plur. is *haec*.

With the enclitic -*ne* the forms are spelt *hicine, haecine, hocine*, etc. *Iste* is similarly strengthened into *istic, istaec, istoc*, or *istuc*.

443. **in conspectum**. Cf. 261.

446. **siet**. Cf. 313 note.

447. **quid ago?** 'what am I to do?' The Pres. Ind. was thus colloquially used instead of a deliberative Subj. In 812 a Pres. Ind. of this sort is directly co-ordinate with a Pres. Subj. Vergil's well-known phrase, A. 2. 322 *quo res summa loco, Panthu? quam prendimus arcem?* is a probable instance of this usage, there being a dramatic propriety in admitting a forcible colloquialism in words uttered under such strong excitement. Cf. infra, 736–7, 1007. For a play on the two senses, the colloquial and the literal, see Pl. Most. 2. 1. 21. For a similar use in Greek, ct. Aesch. P. V. 767, 867, etc.

Cratinum censeo, 'I propose Cratinus.' *Censere* was the word used for moving a resolution in the Senate.

450. **hic**, 'in this case,' or simply 'here.'

451. **restitui in integrum**, 'should be null and void.' Cf. 405 note.

457. **amplius**. *Ampliatio* was the technical term for deferring judgment in a case when more time was needed to collect evidence; *comperendinatio* was the ordinary adjournment to the third day between the first and second part of a trial. Terence, however, was so strict in not making Roman allusions that the coincidence of the words may be accidental.

458. **res magna est**. On the Westminster stage an additional

point is given to these words by the small stature of the Queen's Scholar to whom the part of Crito is by tradition assigned.
    numquid nos vis? Cf. 151 note.
    459. **dudum,** 'before.' Cf. 289 note.
    459-460. **negant redisse,** sc. *servi negant Antiphonem redisse*.
    462. **percontatum.** Supine after *ibo*. Cf. 102 note.
    quoad. Cf. 148 note.
    464. **eccum** = *ecce cum*. Terence uses *eccum* (common), *eccam, eccos, eccas, ecca,* also *eccistam* = *ecce istam*, and *ellum, ellam* = *ecce illum, illam*. Plautus employs also the fuller forms *eccillum, eccillam, eccillud*. In Terence *eccum* may stand by itself, e. g. Andr. 957 *proviso quid agat Pamphilus: atque eccum,* or followed by an Acc., e. g. 600 *sed eccum ipsum,* or with the person referred to following as a subject to a verb, e. g. Ad. 923 *sed eccum Micio egreditur foras.* Cf. 484.
    in tempore, 'at the nick of time.'
    video ... se recipere. Cf. 7 note.

Act II. Scene 4. [III. 1.]

Antipho returns, blaming himself for his faint-hearted flight. He is reassured by Geta that, thanks to Phaedria and Phormio, the interests of Phanium have not been betrayed.

    465. **cum istoc animo es vituperandus,** 'you and your faint heart are much to blame.'
    466. **itane te hinc abisse.** Cf. 153 note.
    467. **tete.** Cf. 172 note.
    468. **consuleres,** 'you should have thought for.' Cf. 299 note.
    469. **propter tuam fidem,** either 'from her confidence in you,' or 'from your assurances:' *fides* meaning either 'belief' or that which produces belief, i. e. 'promises,' 'oaths.'
    poteretur. This form is preferred by Terence to *potiretur*, as also *potītur*: indeed *potĭtur* is only used once by a classical writer, Ov. Her. 14. 113. Terence constructs *potior* three times with an Acc., once with an Abl., infra 830. Cf. Ad. 871, 876. The Augustan construction is the Abl., rarely the Gen. except in the phrase *potīri rerum*.
    471. **iam dudum.** Cf. 289 note.
    qui abieris, 'for your flight :' *qui* is causal.
    474. **subolet,** lit. 'it emits a smell for one,' so 'one gets wind of,' 'has an inkling of:' used impersonally or with a neuter pronoun as subject; only in Plautus and Terence. Cf. Pl. Trin. 615, 698.
    nil etiam, 'nothing at all :' *etiam* is often thus used as an intensive. Cf. 542.

475. nisi, 'only,' 'but.' Cf. 953. This usage seems to be only colloquial.

cessavit eniti, 'slackened his exertions:' *cessare* = 'to flag,' *desinere* = 'to desist.'

476. in, not repeated before *aliis*, as with *cum* 171.

praebuit, sc. *se.*

477. confutavit ... **senem,** 'he utterly quenched the old gentleman when boiling over with rage:' *confutare,* lit. 'to pour cold water into a vessel which is boiling over.'

478. ego quod potui porro. In full the sentence would be, *ego porro feci quod potui facere.*

480. quid eum? 'what about him?' In conversational language an Acc. may be thus loosely used with no verb expressed and probably with none understood. One essential idea of the Acc. is 'limitation,' and so an Acc. may be thus employed to limit the question to the person or thing spoken about. Cf. 755.

aibat = *aiebat.* Terence seems to have used -*ibam* or -*iebam* for the Imperf. of the fourth conjugation indifferently, e.g. Andr. 38 *servibas;* Phor. 83 *serviebat.* The shorter form was sometimes employed by later poets, e. g. *lenibat, nutribant, vestibat* by Vergil; *audibat, mollibat* by Ovid. *Aibam,* etc., probably represents the colloquial pronunciation in the time of Terence. The MSS. are so confused on this point that the reading has usually to be decided by the metre. Cf. 642.

481. The construction is a mixture of *ut aibat, de eius consilio volo facere,* and *aibat de eius consilio sese velle facere.* Cf. Ad. 648 *ut opinor eas non nosse te.*

de eius consilio, 'in accordance with his advice:' cf. the common phrases *de more, de sententia.*

482. metus, Gen. case. Some editors alter the MSS. reading to *metuis,* an archaic form of the Gen. found once in Heaut. 287 *anuis.*

huc salvom, sc. *venire.*

484. eccum. Cf. 464 note.

ab sua palaestra. The term *palaestra,* 'wrestling school,' is here comically applied to the house where Pamphila lives, because Phaedria goes there so regularly. Tr. 'his special place of exercise.'

Act II. Scene 5. [III. 2.]

Phaedria begs Dorio, the owner of Pamphila, to give him three days' grace. Dorio is obdurate : he has an offer for the girl, and will not throw away ready money for tears and promises. 'First come, first served,' is his motto.

NOTES. LINES 475-500. 143

486. **non audio,** 'I won't.' Note the Present used colloquially to express *intention*, as frequently in English and Greek. Cf. 532, 669, 893, 963, 987, 1004.
quin. Cf. 209 note.
omitte me, 'let go of me.'
487. **dicam** is Fut. Indic.
at enim. Cf. 113 note.
490. **mirabar si ... novi,** 'I thought it would be a miracle if you had anything new to say to me;' cf. Andr. 175 *mirabar hoc si sic abiret*. The use of *quicquam* for *quid* implies Dorio s conviction that there was *nothing* new.
491. 'AN. I fear this fellow, lest he should— GE. be patching up some mischief for himself? That is just what I am afraid of.' Antipho was going to say, 'lest he should do some harm to Phaedria.' Geta, interrupting, substitutes significantly 'some mischief for himself, do you mean?' meaning to convey a strong hint to Dorio that he might drive the young men to take violent measures, as Aeschinus did with Sannio in the Adelphi. The words *idem ego vereor* are spoken at Dorio ironically.
suat, lit. 'patch' or 'sew,' whence *sutor* 'a tailor;' only here in metaphorical sense.
492. **hariolare,** 'you are talking nonsense.' The significant change in the meaning of this word, as also of *vaticinari*, shows into what disrepute soothsaying must have fallen before this date. Cf. μαίνομαι and μαντική, Plato Phaedr. 245 B C, Ad. 202.
493. **faeneratum ... dices,** 'you will say that this kindness was richly repaid with interest.' Cf. Ad. 219 *metuisti ... ne non tibi istuc faeneraret?* Both *faeneror* and *faenero* are found; Augustan writers prefer *faeneror*.
logi, Gr. λόγοι, 'mere tattle.' The purer Latin of Terence admits far fewer foreign words than we find in Plautus, and we never meet with actual Greek words, such as οἴχεται, παῦσαι, ἐπιθήκη, πάλιν, all of which occur in the Trinummus.
494. **somnia,** 'moonshine.' Cf. 874.
495. **cantilenam eandem canis,** 'you are singing the same old song,' or 'you are always harping on the same string.'
496. **garri modo,** 'chatter away;' *modo* strengthens the Imperative.
497. **adeon ... esse ... te.** Cf. 153 note.
500. **ut phaleratis dictis** etc. 'that you can lead me on with your "tinsel and spangles," and lead home my girl for nothing.'
phaleratis, from *phalerae*, Gr. φάλαρα, horses' trappings, or decorations like medals worn by soldiers; so the adjective = 'ornamented,' 'fine.'
ducas. A similar sense of *ducere* is found, Andr. 180, 644.

501. **miseritum est**, 'poor fellow.' The full phrase is found Pl. Trin. 430 *me eius miseritum est*. The tense here seems to be an imitation of the so-called 'immediate' Aorist in Greek. In English we should use the Present, 'I pity him.'

veris vincor, 'I can't gainsay the truth.'

quam uterque est similis sui, 'how true to his character each is,' i.e. 'How like Antipho! how like Phaedria!'

502-3. **neque ... malum!** 'and to think of my being confronted with this trouble just when Antipho had been engrossed with a similar anxiety.' In this rendering *neque alia* is taken as = *et non alia*, following Stallbaum. That Antipho was so engrossed is seen from 506. Mr. R. C. Jebb (quoted by B. and W.) translates, 'And then to think that this blow shouldn't have befallen me when A. had some love trouble on hand too.' Wagner changes *neque* to *atque*; Zeune supposes *vellem* to be understood after *neque*; Paumier conjectures *aeque* for *neque*.

autem is often added like Gr. δή as an emphatic particle, especially in questions where some reproach is implied. Cf. 601, 775, 788.

504. **quoi quod amas domi est**, 'you who have at home the object of your love.'

505. Connect *cum malo huius modi* and translate, 'and have never experienced the shock of a trouble like this;' *conflictaris* = *conflictaveris*; cf. Andr. 93 *nam qui cum ingeniis conflictatur eius modi*.

506. **auribus teneo lupum.** A wolf is difficult to hold and dangerous to let go. Donatus quotes the Greek proverb, τῶν ὤτων ἔχω τὸν λύκον· οὔτ' ἔχειν οὔτ' ἀφεῖναι δύναμαι. Cf. 'I've caught a Tartar.'

508. **ipsum ... est**, 'that is exactly my case with him.'

ne ... sies, 'Oh! don't be a scoundrel by halves;' or possibly 'you are afraid of being a scoundrel by halves,' cf. Pl. Pers. 4. 6. 4. 313 note. In Augustan Prose *ne* with Pres. Subj. is only used in *general* prohibitions.

509. **confecit**, 'has he settled?'

511. **ancillam**, sc. *vendere*.

512. **ut me maneat**, 'to give me time.'

cum illo ... fidem, 'to break faith with his customer.'

515. **obtundes**, sc. *aures*, 'will you keep dinning this into me?' *obtundere aures*, 'to beat at the ears,' comes to mean 'to importune,' or 'to annoy by constant repetition,' like the Hellenistic use of ὑπωπιάζειν, St. Luke 18. 5 (B. and W.). Cf. Andr. 348.

exoret sine: *sino* may be followed by a Subj. with or without *ut*, or by an Infin.; cf. 517.

516. 'He too will surely repay you twofold for any service you may have rendered.'

conduplicaverit. A Fut. Perf. is often used by Plautus and Terence to express a future action to be quickly and certainly performed, where in English we should employ a Fut. Simple. Cf. 681, 882, etc.

518. **horunc** = *horum-ce*, cf. 290.

519. **neque ego neque tu,** 'it won't be my doing nor yours either;' i.e. it is Phaedria's fault for not paying over the money.

quod es dignus. In early Latin *dignus* is sometimes constructed with an Acc. neuter pronoun, cf. Plaut. Capt. 969 *non me censes scire quid dignus siem?*

duint. Cf. 123 note.

521. **contra omnia haec.** Some editors, believing that *contra* is not used as a preposition as early as Terence, put a stop after *haec*, understanding *sunt*. But though the adverbial use is much more common, *contra* is found as an undoubted preposition Pl. Ps. 155 *adsistite omnes contra me*, ib. Pers. 1. 1. 13; and it is far more natural to take it as such here and in the parallel passage Ad. 44 *ille contra haec omnia Ruri agere vitam*.

522. **da locum melioribus,** said to have been a formula used by a Consul's lictors in clearing the way.

524. **quam ad,** so all MSS. If the reading be correct, this is a rare instance of *ad* standing after its case. Bentley conjectures *quoad*. Tr. 'unless my memory deceives me, there was assuredly a date once fixed by which you were to pay him.' Cf. Cic. Nat. D. 2. 4 *Senatus, quos ad soleret, referendum censuit.*

factum. Cf. 315 note.

525. **haec,** sc. the date on which the other purchaser appeared.

526. **vanitatis,** 'bad faith.' The quality most prized by the Romans was *gravitas*, a solidity of character on which full reliance could be placed. Opposed to this was *vanitas*, 'fickleness,' 'untrustworthiness.'

dum ob rem, 'provided it pays.' In a similar sense we find *in rem* Andr. 546, and *ex re* 969, in an opposite sense *ab re* Pl. Trin. 238.

527. **sic sum :** etc. ' 'Tis my way. If you like it, deal with me.'

528. **immo enimvero,** 'nay, in very truth.'

532. **dare se dixit** = *daturum se dixit*. We find several instances in Terence where a Pres. Inf. is used instead of a Future Inf., e. g. Andr. 379, 411, 613, Ad. 203, infra 720, 837. Compare the use of the Pres. Ind., 486 note. The idea of *intention* implied in these cases makes the Pres. equivalent to a Future. So also in Plautus, e. g. Most. 3. 1. 99, ib. 5. 2. 21.

533. **mea lege utar** etc. 'I will follow my rule, "first come, first served."'

PHORMIO.

Act II. Scene 6. [III. 3.]

Phaedria, in despair, implores the aid of Geta, who eventually undertakes by some means to procure the money in time.

535. The scansion is doubtful. It might be *quoi mĭnŭs | nihilo est | quŏd hīc si | pote fū | isset* | etc., or *quoi mī | nus nihi | lo est quod hīc | si pote | fuisset* | etc. Wagner lengthens *quod*, making the third foot *quod hic*, but this is improbable.

hic si . . . exorarier, 'if only this three days' grace, could have been wheedled out of him.' In this passage *si* is not strictly conditional, but expresses a wish, exactly as in the corresponding English idiom.

pote. Cf. 379 note.

536. fuerat, Indicative because the promise was a fact, cf. 513.

537. dudum. Cf. 289 note.

dixti. Cf. 198 note.

adiuerit = *adiuverit*. The metre shows that *adiuerit* most nearly represents the pronunciation. Cf. Ennius, apud Cic. Senec. 1. 1 *adiuero*.

538. quin. Cf. 209.

539. equidem, from *quidem*, compounded with the intensive particle *e*, as in *ecastor, edepol, enim*, and perhaps *edurus*. It does not stand for *ego quidem*, and, though more common with the first person singular, is also found with other persons and numbers: e.g. Eun. 956 *atque equidem orante, ut ne hoc faceret, Thaide*; Pl. Pers. 2. 2. 5 *equidem si scis*; Pl. Epid. 4. 2. 33 *adulescentem equidem dicebant emisse*; Sall. Cat. 52. 16 *vanum equidem hoc consilium est*.

540. id unde, sc. *inveniam*; cf. 38 note.

542. Note Hiatus after *itane*. See Introduction, p. 31.

etiam tu hinc abis? 'out with you!' Cf. Eun. 799 *non tu hinc abis?* Ad. 550 *etiam taces?* '*do* be quiet.' This is better than to translate, 'What! are you too going to leave me in the lurch?' *etiam* is often thus used to emphasise questions or imperatives; cf. 474.

543-4. 'Can't I congratulate myself on not having got into trouble about your marriage, without your bidding me now jump out of the frying-pan into the fire for your cousin as well?' *in malo quaerere crucem*, lit. 'when in trouble already to seek for the gallows.'

546. parŭm. A final *m* in Latin was very lightly pronounced, so that *parum* practically = *paru'*. Hence the elision of such syllables.

547. preci. Note that Nom. and Gen. Sing. of this word are nowhere found, Dat. and Acc. Sing. only in ante-Augustan writers. Cf. Andr. 601.

NOTES. LINES 535-568.

549. **tum**, used as a particle of transition, like the English 'then,' especially in questions, as in 541.

550. **cedo.** Cf. 197 note.

552. **pedetemptim**, not *pedetentim*, *templo* not *tento*, etc. Tr. 'cautiously.'

553. **quaere**, 'think.'

554. **faxit.** Cf. 308 note.

quid plus minusve, 'something or other.'

555. **verum enim,** 'but indeed,' *enim* being a particle of emphasis; cf. 113 note. Note that *verum enim* is *verum* strengthened by *enim*, while *enimvero* is *enim* (= indeed) strengthened by *vero*, the former combination being adversative, the latter corroborative.

556. **bona mala,** an effective instance of Asyndeton, i.e. omission of *et*.

557. **opus.** Cf. 440 note.

argenti depends on *quantum*.

triginta minae = over £120; cf. 410 note. The price of accomplished female slaves in these comedies is usually from twenty to thirty minae.

558. **percara.** The prefix *per-* has an intensive force, e. g. *pernimium*, *perscitus*, *perfortiter*, *perliberalis*, common in colloquial speech.

istaec ... est. 'Indeed she is dirt cheap.' Cf. 442 note.

559. **inventas reddam,** more emphatic than *inveniam*. Terence is fond of this idiom, which is probably colloquial. Cf. 974, Andr. 683, etc.

O lepidum! sc. *caput*, a common phrase when some favour has been promised or granted: 'good fellow.'

aufer te hinc, 'off with you;' cf. 566 *hinc modo te amove.*

562. **solus ... amicus.** Donatus quotes from Apollodorus μόνος φιλεῖν γὰρ τοὺς φίλους ἐπίσταται. 'He is the only friend that can befriend one.'

563. **quod opera mea vobis opus sit,** 'which I can do for you.' Here *quod* might be explained as an adverbial Acc., but the phrase is more probably an extension of the construction *quid opus est facto?* etc., *quod* being the subject, *opera mea* being added to complete the sense. Cf. 440 note.

564. **illam,** i. e. Phanium.

ACT III. SCENE 1. [IV. 1.]

Chremes has landed before this Act opens. He tells Demipho how he found the birds flown from Lemnos, and explains the cause of his deep concern at Antipho's unexpected marriage.

568. **adduxtin tecum filiam.** This clause is the antecedent to *qua causa* etc.

570-1. **non manebat ... meam neglegentiam,** 'did not wait for my negligent delay :' i. e. the girl was growing older and older while Chremes still was absent.

familia, 'the household.' As slaves frequently constituted a large majority of a Roman household, *familia* was often used when the slaves were wholly or chiefly meant.

572. **illi** = *illic*. Cf. 91 note.
578. **condicionem,** 'match,' in the matrimonial sense.
580. **sit.** The subject is the young lady implied in *condicio*.
583. **intercedet familiaritas,** 'there shall be a good understanding between us.'
584. **opus est scito.** Cf. 440 note.
585. **aliqua,** sc. *via*, 'somehow.' Cf. 566, 746.
586. **me excutiam,** 'clear myself out.' Cf. Hor. Od. 3. 9. 19 *si flava excutitur Chloe.* Eun. 358 *homo quatietur certe cum dono foras.* *Excutio me* sometimes means 'I shake out my pockets' (*sinus*), to show that I have no stolen goods.

587. **nam ... meus,** 'for I have nothing but myself to call my own,' implying, 'I am the only thing in my own house I *dare* call my own.'

589. **neque defetiscar** etc., 'and I will not slacken in my efforts until I have actually accomplished ...'

usque adeo ... donec. Cf. Andr. 662 *orare usque adeo donec perpulit*.

experirier. Cf. 92 note.

ACT III. SCENE 2. [IV. 2.]

Geta narrates with admiration the quickness of Phormio in understanding the new turn events had taken, and his readiness to co-operate in the scheme to get the required money.

591. **hominem,** added colloquially to *neminem* for emphasis: cf. Ad. 259.

592. **venio ... ut dicerem.** Cf. 117 note.
593. **argentum opus esse.** Cf. 440 note.
et id ... fieret, 'and how it all happened.'
594. **vixdum.** Cf. 329 note.
intellexerat, 'he saw it all at a glance.' Note the force of the pluperfect.
595. **quaerebat,** 'he was asking for.'
596. **tempus,** 'opportunity.'
600. **eccum ipsum.** Cf. 464 note.
quis est ulterior, 'who is that behind?' Chremes is here standing behind Demipho.

attat, an interjection denoting apprehensive recognition of some danger, e. g. 963, Andr. 125 *percussit ilico animum : attat hoc illud est.*

601. sed quid pertimui autem belua? 'but yet why was I such a jackass as to be scared?' belua, 'a dolt,' 'an ass;' cf. Pl. Trin. 952.

autem. Cf. 503 note.

602. an quia = *an pertimui quia.*

603. duplici spe utier, 'to have two strings to my bow.' Cf. 92 note. Gr. ἐπὶ δυοῖν ἀγκύραιν ὁρμεῖν.

604. petam, 'I will try to get the money.' a primo, 'at first;' cf. 642.

605. hunc hospitem, 'this new-comer.' Geta can use *hinc* and *hunc* with reference to Demipho and Chremes respectively, because he indicates to the audience by gesture the object of his remarks.

ACT III. SCENE 3. [IV. 3.]

Geta now puts his scheme into execution. He tells Demipho and Chremes that in their interest he has sounded Phormio, and has found him open to the following arrangement. On receipt of thirty minae the parasite will give up all legal proceedings and marry Phanium himself. To this Chremes scarcely persuades his brother by offering to provide the money from his wife's income.

607. expecto, 'I am waiting to see.'

610. volup est, 'I am delighted:' *volup*, an adverb, usually in the phrase *volup est* opposed to *aegre est*, from root VOL- whence *voluptas*, *Volupia* the goddess of pleasure, etc. The form *volupe* which appears in some MSS. is incorrect. In Terence only here and Hec. 857, fairly common in Plautus, never in Augustan writers. Cf. Gr. ἐλπίς.

credo. Cf. 255.

quid agitur? 'how goes it?' a common form of salutation, like *quid fit?*

611. 'There are many changes here, as is usual when one first comes home—very many.'

compluria, the older form of *complura*, which accounts for the Gen. *complurium*. Neither Plautus nor Terence use *pluria*, though Gellius mentions it as the original form.

614. circumiri, 'to be circumvented:' so also *circumvenire*; in English 'to get round a man.'

id . . . commodum, 'I was talking with him about that just now.'

commodum, used in the comic writers as a temporal adverb, either = *opportune*, 'in the nick of time,' e. g. Pl. Trin. 400, or = *modo*, 'just now,' as here ; only ante- and post-classical. Gr. ἀρτίως.

615. nam hercle. *Nam* is thus joined to words of asseveration, not

giving any logical confirmation of the preceding statement, but as a connective particle with what follows. In English 'and indeed.' Cf. 113 note, Ad. 190.

agitans, 'turning the matter over.'

618. **qui Phormio?** 'what Phormio?' Donaldson, Varr. p. 381, following Kritz, and apparently Madvig, § 88, obs. 1, maintain that *quis* and *quid* merely ask for the name, but *qui* and *quod* (interrogative) inquire respecting the kind, condition, or quality of the person or thing. The truth seems to be that in many cases the substantival use of *quis* and the adjectival use of *qui* are attended with this distinction of meaning, which naturally arises from the form of the sentence, e. g. Eun. 823–4 *TH. Quis fuit igitur? PY. Iste Chaerea. TH. Qui Chaerea?* But that this distinction is not inherent in the actual words *quis* and *qui* is clear from the fact that *quis est Phormio? quid est remedium?* would require the same answer as *qui Phormio? quod remedium?* and that Cicero uses *qui* before a consonant, *quis* before a vowel. In many cases where *quis* seems to be used adjectivally the irregularity is only apparent, e. g. And. 965 *quis homo est?* 'who is there?' is literally 'who is the man?' Verg. G. 2. 178 *quis color*, 'what is its distinguishing colour?' Cf. 990–1.

is qui istam—, sc. *nobis obtrusit* or some such words: *istam =* Phanium. Translate, 'the man by whom that girl'—

620. **prendo hominem solum,** 'I button-hole the fellow.'

621–2. 'Why do you not see how we can settle this matter between us amicably rather than by strife:' *videre ut* may be followed by Ind., e. g. Verg. A. 6. 779, cf. 358 note. Here the Subj. is required by the idea of contingency.

sic, i. e. as I am about to suggest.

623. **liberalis,** 'a gentleman.' Cf. 815.

fugitans litium, 'shy of law-suits.' When participles from transitive verbs are used as pure adjectives they can be constructed with an objective Genitive, e. g. *negotii gerens*, 'carrying on a business,' etc.; cf. Madv. § 289.

624. **modo**, 'just now,' when qualifying *unus* it usually stands second.

625. **auctores . . . daret,** 'advised him to turn the girl out of doors.'

628. **iam id exploratum est,** 'he has had good advice on that point.'

sudabis satis, 'you'll have a hot enough time of it.'

630. **verum pono . . .,** 'but granted that . . .'

at tandem tamen, 'yet after all.' For the pleonasm cf. 80 note.

631. **non capitis** etc., ' 'tis not a question of life or death.'
632. **mollirier.** Cf. 92 note, infra 640.
633-4. **quid vis dari tibi in manum?** 'what will you take in cash?' 'To pay cash' is *repraesentare*.
635. **haec hinc facessat,** 'the girl should take herself off:' *se* is understood. The phrase is classical, but the fact that it is only used in sentences directly or indirectly imperatival points to its colloquial origin.
   sies. Cf. 313 note.
636. **satin illi di sunt propitii?** 'is the fellow in his senses?' Madness was always regarded as a divine visitation.
638. **ut est ille bonus vir,** 'so good a man is he.'
   commutabitis etc., a colloquial phrase = 'to have words about a thing.'
640. **non potuit,** impersonal ; cf. 303 note.
642. **insanibat,** 'raved.' Cf. 480 note.
   cedo. Cf. 197.
643. **nimium quantum lubuit,** 'he wanted a great deal too much ;' cf. Gr. πλεῖστον ὅσον, θαυμαστὸν ὅσον. Similar phrases are *mirum quantum, incredibile quantum.* Bentley, followed by others, reads *nimium quantum. CH. Quantum? die.* But there is no MSS. authority for the change.
644. **talentum magnum,** 'a whole Attic talent.' There was a small Sicilian talent. Cf. 393 note. Pl. Most. 3. 1. 110, ib. 4. 2. 913.
   immo malum hercle! a *double entendre : malum dare* = ' to inflict punishment,' but Demipho is also referring to the preceding *magnum,* which he alters to *malum,* sc. *dabo,* ' a great talent! I'll give him a great thrashing.'
645. **quod adeo,** 'the very thing which.' Cf. 389 note.
   quid si etc. This sentence is elliptical. The full sense would be, ' if he were to portion out an only daughter, what could he do more ?'
   locaret, sc. *in matrimonium,* or *nuptum ;* cf. 752.
646. **rettulit,** so spelt in A. Cf. 21, 723 notes.
647. **non suscepisse,** 'that he did not rear one.' The father formally acknowledged a new-born child and undertook to bring it up as his own by raising it from the ground, when it had been laid before him : *tollere* is also used in this sense, e.g. Andr. 219. Cf. 967, 1007.
648. **ut ad pauca redeam,** 'to cut a long story short.'
651. **fuerat.** The Pluperfect because referring to a time antecedent to that implied in *volui.* The English idiom does not admit of it. Tr. 'as was right and fair.'

653. Tr. 'that a poor girl is given in slavery, not wedlock, to a rich man.'

in servitutem is substituted for *in matrimonium*.

ad ditem, not *diti*, because there is an idea of sending to the rich man's house. The position of a wife depended materially upon her dowry. See the relations of Nausistrata to Chremes; Pl. Trin. 688–691, etc.

655. qui. Cf. 123 note.

657. accipio, 'I am getting.' Cf. 447 note.

660. Incertŭs sum. Cf. 943, Introduction, p. 29.

661. si animam debet, 'if he is over head and ears in debt:' Gr. καὶ αὐτὴν τὴν ψυχὴν ὀφείλει.

ager oppositus est pignori, 'some land has been mortgaged.'

663. oiei, an exclamation, cf. *hui*.

664. ne clama. This archaic construction is not common in Terence, and disappeared altogether in later Latin, except in the poets, or as an intentional archaism, e. g. Liv. 3. 2. Cf. 803.

repetīto. All MSS give *petito*, but another syllable is necessary for the metre.

665. pluscula, 'a little extra;' *plusculum* as a substantive is classical. Note the diminutives *aediculae, ancillula, pluscula*.

667. pone sane, 'put down, if you please;' *sane* is often thus used with Imperatives in colloquial language.

668. sescentas, Gr. μυρίας, the word commonly used for an indefinitely large number, as in English 'a hundred' or 'a thousand.' Cf. Pl. Trin. 791 *sescentae causae*, Cic. Verr. 2. 1. 47 *possum sescenta decreta proferre*.

dīcas. Cf. 127.

669. nil do, 'I won't give a farthing.' For the tense see 447 note.

ut inrideat. Cf. 304 note.

670–1. The order is, *tu modo fac ut filius* (sc. Antipho) *ducat illam* (sc. Chremes' daughter) *quam nos volumus*.

673. eicitur, sc. Phanium.

674. quantum potest, 'as quickly as possible,' a common phrase, *fieri* being probably understood; *potest* is impersonal. Cf. 897.

face. Cf. 309 note.

675. illam, sc. Phanium, hanc, sc. *quae sponsa est mihi*, cf. 657.

676. illi, sc. my betrothed's relations, so *illis* in 677.

677. iam accipiat, 'let him have the money at once.'

repudium renuntiet, 'should inform them that the engagement is broken off;' *repudium* is the dissolution of the marriage contract by one of the parties to it, *divortium* is a separation by mutual consent.

Consequently *repudium* is often used, as here, of persons engaged but not married.

679. **opportune adeo**, 'most luckily;' cf. 389 note.
680. **Lemni**, Locative case. Terence also uses *in Lemno* 873, 1004.
681. **dixero**. Cf. 516 note.

ACT III. SCENE 4. [IV. 4.]

Antipho, who was entirely in the dark as to the scheme between Phormio and Geta, had overheard with amazement and dismay the arrangement by which he was to lose his beloved Phanium. As soon as the old gentlemen are gone he fiercely assails Geta, who has some difficulty in assuring him that the whole affair is only a temporary ruse to get the money, and that there is no real cause to fear the actual accomplishment of the projected marriage between Phanium and Phormio.

682. **emunxi argento senes**, 'I have cleaned the old gentlemen out of their money.' Cf. Gr. ἀπομύσσεσθαι, applied to a drivelling old man.

683. **satin id est?** etc. 'Is that all?' 'I really don't know: it was all my orders.' Geta purposely misapplies Antipho's question to the amount of money demanded. Literally *satin id est?* = 'are you satisfied with that?'

684. **verbero**, 'you scoundrel.' Cf. *mastigia*, Ad. 781.

685. **ergo** is often used as an emphasising particle, especially in questions and commands. 'What then do you mean?' Cf. 755 note, 882, 948, 984, 995. I.iv. 9. 31. 16 *itaque ergo*.

quid ego narrem? Cf. 122 note.

686. **ad restim res redit**, 'I have only a halter left,' i.e. the only thing left is to hang myself. Cf. Pl. Trin. 537 *ut ad incitas redactus est*.

restim, Abl. *reste*. **redit** = *rediit* as often, cf. 55, etc.

687. **ut**, introducing a wish as in 711, 773.

688. **malis exemplis**, 'with condign punishments;' *exemplum* was specially used for a 'method of punishment.'

689. Here the MSS. read *huic mandes quod quidem recte curatum velis*, which cannot stand after *si quid velis* and is almost certainly a gloss from Ad. 372 *huic mandes, si quid recte curatum velis*. The reading in the text is found in the margin of E and F. Tr. 'Here's a pilot to take one out of smooth water on to a reef.'

690. **utibile** = *utile*, only here in Terence, found in Plautus, e.g. Trin. 748, not Augustan.

692. **cedo**. Cf. 197 note.

694. **non enim.** Cf. 113 note.
696. **in nervom.** Cf. 325 note.
701. **tandem,** 'after all,' so used Lucr. 5. 137. An easier reading would be *tamen*, but no MS. gives it.
702. **vocandi,** ' for issuing invitations.'
705. **monstra** [*monestra*, fr. *moneo*]. Omens, termed generically *auspicia, auguria*, were divided by the Romans into five classes—

(1) *ex caelo*, e. g. thunder and lightning.

(2) *ex avibus*, which gave omens by their note (*oscines*), or by their flight (*alites*).

(3) *ex tripudiis*, i. e. from the feeding of the sacred chicken.

(4) *ex quadrupedibus*, only used for private divination.

(5) *ex diris*, i. e. any portentous event, not otherwise classified; such were called *prodigia, portenta*.

Tr. 'how many things have proved ominous to me since that event!'
postilla. Cf. 347 note.

706. **introiit** scans as a dactyl, *intrŏĭt*, the final syllable being first contracted, cf. 55, and then shortened by the Iambic Law. See Introduction, p. 27. A black dog or cat has usually been considered 'uncanny.' Mephistopheles appears to Faust as a black poodle.

707. **inpluvium,** also '*conpluvium*,' 'the skylight,' a quadrangular opening in the roof of a Roman atrium, through which smoke went out and rain came in; also sometimes the square basin sunk in the floor which received the rain. The second foot must be scanned as a proceleusmatic, *pĕr ĭnplŭvĭ* | *um*. To avoid this many editors print *in* for *per*.

708. **gallina cecinit,** 'a hen crowed,' sc. like a cock. This was an omen, according to Donatus, that the wife would survive the husband.

708-9. **hariolus, haruspex,** synonymous terms for a soothsayer who interpreted omens from the entrails of victims (Sans. *hirâ* = entrails). The art soon fell into disrepute among the educated classes, cf. 492 note. Note that the whole system of omens at Rome had a practical bearing. The signs warned men to do or not to do some act, and so the auspices were taken or soothsayers consulted before any undertaking of importance in public or private life. Cf. Hor. Od. 3. 27. 1-7—

Impios parrae recinentis omen
Ducat, et praegnans canis, aut ab agro
Rava decurrens lupa Lanuvino
Fetaque vulpes:
Rumpat et serpens iter institutum,
Si per obliquum similis sagittae
Terruit mannos. sqq.

aliquid is only found as a correction in E, Eugraphius reading *quid*. Otherwise the MSS. read *autem*, which is in itself awkward and leaves *negoti* without a construction. Many editors place a colon after *vetuit* and assume the loss of two half-verses between *incipere* and *quae*. But of this there is no trace in the MSS. or the Scholiasts, and it seems the least of the difficulties to read *aliquid*.

711. **me vide,** ' look to me,' ' trust to me.' Cf. Andr. 350, Pl. Trin. 808.

ACT III. SCENE 5. [IV. 5.]

The old gentlemen re-appear with the money for Phormio. Chremes is manifestly apprehensive of some trickery, but Demipho is confident that no one will get the better of him. Chremes is also anxious that Nausistrata should be sent to break the news to Phanium, and his brother somewhat impatiently assents.

713. **ne quid verborum duit,** ' that he practise no trickery on us ; ' *verba dare* = ' to cheat.'

duit. Cf. 123 note.

714. **hoc ... a me,** 'I will never rashly part with it,' i. e. the money.

715. **commemorabo,** 'I will formally recite,' i. e. before the witnesses.

716. **opus facto est.** Cf. 440 note.

lubido, ' caprice.'

717. **si ... instabit,** 'if that other girl (cf. 657) puts more pressure on him.'

719. **ut conveniat hanc,** ' to visit her,' i. e. Phanium. This is the classical construction of *convenire* in the above sense.

720. The order is *dicat nos dare eam nuptum* (Supine) *Phormioni*. For *dare* cf. 532 note.

721. **familiarior,** ' more intimately connected.' Cf. 851.

723. **malum,** ' the plague ; ' thus used interjectionally, cf. Ad. 544 *quid hoc, malum, infelicitatis?* infra 948 and 976 where there is a relative clause appended.

quid tua id refert? ' what does it matter to you ? ' The comic poets prefer *refert* to *interest*; Cicero much prefers *interest*. Augustan writers construct *refert* with *ad* and Acc. more often than with Gen.

724. **te** is here used in a general sense, like ' you ' in English. Cf. Ad. 30 etc.

725. **quoque** is an almost certain interpolation, as shown by the metre.

726. mulier ... convenit, 'one woman gets on better with another.'
727. illas, sc. his wife and daughter from Lemnos, cf. 571-2.

ACT III. SCENE 6. [V. 1.]

Chremes is startled by the sudden appearance of Sophrona, a servant of his Lemnian wife, from Demipho's house. He learns from her the death of her mistress and the marriage of Phanium to Antipho. At first he fails to identify his own daughter with Phormio's ward, and thinks that his nephew like himself must have married two wives: but the confusion is soon removed and his joy is unbounded.

730. suasum, 'advice,' only ante- and post-classical.
732. nam quae = *quaenam*, 'why? who?'
a fratre, 'from my brother's house:' a common idiom, e. g. 795. etc.
733. infirmas, 'insecure,' because divorce was so easy, and parental authority so great, that no marriage could be safely depended on without the father's consent.
735. edepol, 'by Pollux,' shorter form *pol* 747. The prefix is from the interjection *e*, as in *e-castor,* and perhaps a syncopated vocative of *deus*.
736. quid ago? Cf. 447 note, and 737.
737. adeo...maneo...cognosco, 'am I to approach,' etc. Note that this use of the Pres. Ind. for Pres. Subj. is usually in animated speech, making the effect more vivid. Cf. 447 note.
741. istorsum (*isto-vorsum*), 'that way.' Chremes is now standing between Sophrona and the house.
742. appellassis, usually considered as syncopated from *appellaveris,* as *excessis* And. 790, from *excesseris;* cf. Zumpt, § 161. But Madv. § 115 f. and Roby §§ 291-3 consider both these forms, like *faxo, ausim,* etc., to be remnants of an archaic Future in *-so* (Ind.), *-sim* Subj.; while King and Cookson, pp. 462-3, hold *amasso, amassim,* etc., to be conjunctive and optative forms of the sigmatic aorist. In Plautus is found an Inf. in *-assere,* e. g. *impetrassere.* Cf. 308 note. It may be noted that here the Perf. Subj. would be the tense naturally expected. Livy uses *adclarassis,* 1. 18.
743. st! 'hist.' This exclamation scans as a long syllable.
744. conclusam, the word applied to a wild beast in a cage. Tr. 'I have a ferocious wife caged up there.'
745. perperam, 'falsely,' used by Cicero; Gr. πέρπερος.
746. effutiretis, 'should blurt it out;' connected with *futilis, fundo.*
porro, 'afterwards,' 'later on.' The more remote in a succession of events seems the essential idea. Cf. 923, 937, 1025.

aliqua. Cf. 585 note.

747. istoc, 'on that account,' like *eo*.

751. quae essem, 'since I was,' *quae* causal. male factum! 'what a pity!' a very cool expression of grief.

752. nuptum locavi. Cf. 645, 720.

753. dominus, in the absence of Demipho his son was 'master.' Note Hiatus after *Hem!* as after *Au!* in 754, 803.

754. Au! a female exclamation, usually of deprecation, e. g. 803: Gr. ἰού. The text, following Bentley, omits *habet* after *uxores, metri gratia*. Some editors omit *is* or *obsecro*.

The consternation of Chremes at finding that his nephew had, as it seemed, so early copied his uncle's bigamy, is very humorous.

For ellipse of the verbs here and in 755 see 38 note.

755. quid illam alteram, 'what about that other one?' haec ergo est, 'this is the very girl.' Cf. 685 note.

756. composito factum est, 'it was done by arrangement.' amans, 'her lover,' here a pure substantive.

757. di vostram fidem, 'good heavens.' Acc. of exclamation, cf. 351 note.

758. offendi, 'I have accidentally found,' lit. 'stumbled on.'

759. 'That she has been wedded to the man I wished, and is loved as I wished.' Chremes is speaking to himself, and so there is no ambiguity in omitting *gnatam*, which some editors substitute for *amari* the reading of A.

761. haec sola, sc. Sophrona. The reading is doubtful. If *hic solus* be right, Antipho must be meant.

762. quid opus facto sit. Cf. 440 note.

763. oppido. Cf. 317.

765. scibit. Terence uses *scibo* for 1st pers., *scies* for 2nd pers. (except in Heaut. 996 and perhaps Eun. 805), *scibit* for 3rd pers.

The MSS. read *sequere me: cetera intus* (or *intus cetera*) *audies*, which will not scan. The insertion of *tu* seems more satisfactory than to change *audies* to *audiemus* or *audietis*. The line then becomes an Octonarius, as the last line of Ad. 4. 5 (712), which also follows Septenarii.

ACT IV. SCENE 1. [V. 2.]

Demipho returns from paying the money to Phormio in a very bad temper, which is not improved by Geta's expression of doubt as to the fulfilment of the compact. Geta himself is by no means easy with regard to his own prospects of escaping punishment.

766. nostrapte. Cf. 172.
ut malos expediat esse, 'that it pays to be a rogue;' cf. Heaut. 388 *expedit bonas esse vobis*.

767. dici nos bonos studemus. Note that in Augustan Latin a predicative word following an Infin. and referring to a subject in the Nom. is itself in the Nom., e.g. *Bibulus studet fieri consul*. Cf. Ad. 504, Madv. § 393.

768. ita fugias, ne praeter casam, sc. *fugias*, 'in running away, don't pass the house' (i.e. your master's); a proverb applicable to a runaway slave, something like 'don't jump out of the frying-pan into the fire,' or 'don't go farther and fare worse.' Demipho means that in trying to get out of one trouble he is running the risk of a worse. *Casa*, properly a 'hut,' 'cottage,' might be easily applied in slaves' slang to the master's house, 'the diggings.' Another interpretation is, 'in running away, don't pass your house,' which is the safest place for you. But the application of this to Demipho's present circumstances is not obvious. Mr. Stock renders 'More haste, less speed.'
nonne. Cf. 119 note.

769. etiam argentum est ultro obiectum, 'we have actually thrown money to him as well,' i.e. like a sop to Cerberus. Cf. Verg. A. 6. 420-1 *melle soporatam et medicatis frugibus offam obicit*. For *ultro* cf. 360 note.

770. qui. Cf. 123 note.
771. qui recta prava faciunt, 'who confound right with wrong.'
772. ut, 'so that.' Demipho continues his sentence from 771.
illi = *illic*, 'in that affair.' Cf. 91 note.

773. modo ut etc. 'I only hope that we may be able to get out of it by this plan of his marrying her:' *discedi*, cf. 1047, Andr. 148 : *possiet*, impersonal; for the archaic form see 313 note. The marriage of Phormio with Phanium is of course meant. For *ut* introducing a wish see 687, 711.

774. haud scio ... an mutet animum, 'I really don't know whether he won't change his mind.' The English idiom requires a negative in the second clause, because *haud scio an* suggests 'probably,' but 'I don't know whether' suggests 'probably not.'
ut homo est, 'being human;' a thoroughly Terentian touch.
ut, 'seeing that.'

775. mutet autem ? ' ' what ? change ? ' Cf. 503 note.
777. ista, i. e. Phanio; hanc, i. e. Nausistratam.

778. de iurgio siletur, 'not a word about the quarrel.'
779. haec, sc. Phanium.
780. in eodem luto haesitas, 'you are sticking in the same mire.'
vorsuram solves, 'you will have to pay compound interest··'
vorsuram facere='to borrow from one man to pay another.' Geta means that he has got the money for Phaedria at the expense of a new complication about Phanium, for which he will have to pay the penalty.
781. in diem abiit, 'is put off for the moment.' Cf. *in diem vivere.*
plagae crescunt, 'my score of stripes is running up.'
783. eius, sc. Nausistrata, see stage direction.

Act IV. Scene 2. [V. 3.]

Demipho re-appears from his brother's house escorting Nausistrata, who has consented to inform Phanium of the proposed arrangements. Nausistrata is eloquent on the feebleness of Chremes as compared with her father.

784. age dum. Cf. 594 note.
786. re dudum, 'just now with your money.' Cf. 681, and for *dudum* 289 note.
787. factum volo, 'you are very welcome,' lit. 'I wish it done.' Distinguish *factum volo*, 'I am glad it is so;' *factum velim*, 'I hope it may be so;' *factum vellem*, 'I wish it were so.' So too *factum nolo*, etc.
788. quid autem? 'why, what do you mean?' Cf. 503 note.
790. statim, 'regularly,' only ante-classical in this case.
The subject of *capiebat* is Nausistrata's father.
vir viro quid praestat! 'what a difference there is in men!'
791. 'Yes, two talents, and that when prices were much lower.'
792. quid haec videntur? scilicet. This question and answer are obscure. The meaning may be, (1) 'What do you think of this?' 'Of course you are right:' or (2) 'What! do you think so?' (referring to Demipho's *hui!* of admiration). 'Of course I do.' Hence Colman's translation, 'What! are you surprised?'· 'Prodigiously.' In any case Demipho's *scilicet* is not likely to be either ironical or absent, as supposed by some, since he is very anxious to pay Nausistrata every attention.
natum, the reading of Λ_2 is more characteristic of Nausistrata than *natam*.
793. parce sodes, 'please spare yourself.' Cf. 103 note.
794. cum illa, sc. *conloqui.* Demipho expected a scene.
795. abs te. Cf. 732 note.

Act IV. Scene 3. [V. 3.]

As Demipho and Nausistrata approach the house, Chremes comes out in great excitement from an interview with his daughter. He wants of course to stop any further proceedings with reference to Phanium, but finding Nausistrata with Demipho he cannot explain matters. Demipho gets impatient and Nausistrata suspicious at his inexplicable conduct and manifest agitation, and only with great difficulty does Chremes get his wife safely back into her own house, so that he can impart to his brother the news which he has been bursting to tell.

796. **nollem datum.** Cf. 787 note.
797. **paene,** sc. *dixi*. Cf. 440 note.
798. **iam recte.** 'it's all right.' Cf. 812.

quid tu? introduces a new point like *quid?* cf. 64 note, and *quid ais?* cf. 199 note.

istac = Phanium; **hanc** = Nausistrata.
799. **qui,** 'how?' Cf. 123 note.
800. **'est cordi,'** 'is dear to,' a common phrase.

nostra, sc. *refert*. Cf. 940.

801. **sic erit,** 'so it will prove:' an idiomatic form of confident asseveration which may refer to the past, e. g. Heaut. 1014 *subditum se suspicatur. CH. Subditum, ain tu? SO. Sic erit*, the present as here, and of course the future, e. g. Ad. 182.

803. **Au!** with Hiatus, as in 754.

ne nega. Cf. 664.

804. **aliud dictum est,** 'was wrongly given.'

hoc tu errasti, 'it was this which misled you:' *hoc* Acc. Cf. Andr. 498 *teneo quid erret*.

806. **miror quid siet,** 'I wonder what it's all about.' Nausistrata has been observing with growing suspicion her husband's manifest perturbation and his anxiety to stop any conversation on the subject. Cf. 313 note.

807. **ita . . . ut,** thus used in strong asseverations, literally, 'may Jupiter so preserve me according as . . . .' Cf. Roby 715 f.

809. **aut scire aut nescire hoc,** 'know the truth or falsehood of this matter.' That Nausistrata should be present at any enquiry of the sort is of course what Chremes most dreads.

811. **vin satis . . . esse?** 'do you wish me to ask no further questions about it?'

quid. Cf. 798 note.

NOTES. LINES 796-830.

illa filia, Abl., cf. 137 note. Demipho, in the presence of Nausistrata, thus alludes to Chremes' Lemnian daughter.

812. **hanc igitur mittimus?** 'Then are we to drop her?' i.e. give up our plan of marrying her to Antipho. For the mood see 447 note: here *mittimus* is co-ordinate with *maneat*.

813. **quid ni?** 'certainly.' illa, i.e. Phanium.

814. **in omnis**, 'for all parties.'

815. **perliberalis**, 'very lady-like.' Cf. 558 note.

817. **di nos respiciunt**, 'it is quite providential.' Cf. 854.

818. **potuit**, 'was it possible.' Cf. 303 note.

ACT IV. SCENE 4. [V. 4.]

In a short soliloquy Antipho contrasts his cousin's happiness, secured by thirty minae, and his own wretchedness, from which there seems no escape.

820. **ut....habent**, 'considering the state of my own affairs.'

fratri, sc. *patrueli*, a cousin on his father's side: cf. use of ἀδελφός.

821. **scitum**, 'sensible.' Cf. 110 note.

822. **sient**, Subjunctive, because the statement is general and indefinite.

paulo, 'easily;' more commonly with a word of comparison, or *ante*, *post*, etc.

mederi usually governs a dative, and this may merely be a case of Inverse Attraction. See, however, Verg. A. 7. 756 *sed non Dardaniae medicari cuspidis ictum Evaluit*, contrasted with ib. G. 2. 135, Ter. Andr. 831, 944.

823. **simul** = *simul ac*. Cf. Liv. 4. 5, etc.

825. **si hoc celetur**, Subjunctive, because he does not think it will remain secret. Cf. Andr. 568-9.

sin patefit. Indicative, because he believes it will be revealed. Note that when *facio* is compounded with prepositions it modifies the vowel of the stem and forms its Passive regularly, e. g. *inficior*; when connected with other parts of speech the *a* is not modified and the Passive is in *fio*, such not being regarded as true compounds.

827. **habendae**, 'of keeping,' like Gr. ἔχειν. Cf. 880.

ACT IV. SCENE 5. [V. 5.]

Phormio enters, congratulating himself on the successful result of his plans for Phaedria. He now intends to leave town in order to enjoy a few days' quiet drinking.

830. **propria ut poteretur**, 'should gain her as his own,' i.e. should

L

make her his wife, which could not have been done had she remained a slave. For *poteretur* cf. 469.

Phaedriā. The final *a* in Greek names is usually long in Terence, except in dissyllables, e. g. Getă.

emissa est manu, 'she has been freed.'

831-2. **otium ab senibus,** 'some peace from the old gentlemen.'

aliquot hos sumam dies, 'I will take these next few days,' sc. as a holiday.

833. **quid ais? quid?** 'what now? what do you mean?'

835. **partis tuas.** Cf. 215-17.

836. **suas,** sc. *partes.* Cf. 266-6.

rursum, 'in return' (*re-vorsum*).

837. **ire.** Cf. 532 note.

Sunium, the southern promontory of Attica. There was in the deme a prosperous town, owing to the silver mines of Laurium, a strong fort built during the Peloponnesian war, and a celebrated temple of Athena overlooking the sea.

838. **emptum,** Supine.

dudum, 'just now,' cf. 665.

839. **conficere,** 'that I am making short work of.'

840. **ostium concrepuit.** Folding doors were in general use among the Greeks and Romans, hence the pl. *fores, valvae.* These seem to have opened either outwards or inwards, and so it was customary for a person leaving a house to rattle or knock the door as a warning to those without. This noise is usually described as in the text. The door is said *crepare,* or *concrepare,* Gr. ψοφεῖν. Hence some have thought (see Ramsay, Mostellaria 2. 2. 23-5) that *crepare* merely refers to the creaking of the hinges, but Ad. 788, and Most. 2. 2. 74 5, seem decidedly against this view. A person knocking (usually) from without is said, *pellere, pulsare, pultare,* less commonly *percutere,* Gr. κόπτειν, κρούειν, ἁράσσειν. Tr. 'there's a noise at your door.'

abs te, 'at your house.' Cf. 188, 732 notes.

ACT IV. SCENE 6. [V. 6.]

Geta suddenly issues from the house of Demipho in great excitement. By some adroit eavesdropping he has learnt the secret about Chremes' Lemnian daughter and her identity with Phanium. All this he relates to Phormio and Phaedria.

841. **O Fortuna, O Fors Fortuna,** 'O luck! O great good luck!' Fors Fortuna, the goddess of good luck, had a separate temple on the right bank of the Tiber distinct from that of Fortuna: the verbs therefore are plural. The Asyndeton is natural in such excited speech.

842. **meo ero,** Dat. commodi.

843. **quidnam hic sibi volt?** 'whatever does the fellow mean?' a colloquial phrase frequent in Terence. The ordinary meaning of *velle aliquid alicui* is 'to want' or 'to wish something for some one.' Cf. 946.

844. **mihi cesso,** 'I am wasting my time,' lit. 'I am loitering to my own injury.'

umerum. Cf. 39 note.

pallio. Slaves out of doors sometimes wore a coarse outer garment, the lower fold of which would be thrown over the shoulder when they wanted to make haste.

845. **contigerint.** We should have expected *ut quae contigerint sciat*, or *ut haec quae contigerunt sciat*. The Subjunctive may perhaps depend on the idea of the character of the news to be imparted rather than the mere fact.

847. **em tibi!** 'there you are again!' Cf. 52 note.

848. It seems to have been a common practical joke to delay slaves when in a hurry, in order to get them into trouble. It is a stock incident in Terentian comedy. Cf. 195, Ad. 321 etc.

849. **pergit hercle,** 'he's going on, by Jove.'

numquam tu odio tuo me vinces, 'you will never get the better of me with all your annoyance.' *odium* = importunate insolence, cf. Hor. Sat. 1. 7. 6, Hec. 123, 154.

850. **vapula,** 'go and be hanged,' lit. 'beaten,' a colloquial phrase.

verbero. Cf. 684.

851. **familiariorem,** 'one of the family.' Cf. 721.

852. **actutum,** 'immediately,' common in Plautus, but occurs only once in Cicero and once in Livy.

853. For scansion of *O* see 259 note, Introduction, p. 31.

quantum est qui vivont. Cf. the common phrase *quicquid est deorum*. Tr. 'the happiest man alive.'

homo hominum, thus doubled for the sake of emphasis.

854. **ab dis solus diligere.** Cf. Andr. 973 *solus est quem diligant di*.

855. **qui,** 'how?' 'why?' Cf. 123 note, 878.

856. **satin est?** 'is it not enough?' Cf. 119 note.

delibutum gaudio, 'over head and ears in joy:' lit. 'smeared over.' Cf. Cic. Rosc. Amer. § 135.

enicas. Cf. 384.

857. **cedo.** Cf. 197 note.

858. **tu quoque aderas?** 'Oh! you here too?' a colloquial use of the Imperfect, 'expressing surprise at the *present* discovery of a fact already existing.' Allen and Greenough, Lat. Gr. § 277 *d*. Cf. 945, Hor. Od. 1. 27. 19 *quanta laborabas Charybdi*.

accipe, em! 'listen, here goes!'

859. recta, sc. *via*.

862. **gynaeceum**, Gr. γυναικεῖον. The women's apartments were at the back of the house, beyond the αὐλή or central hall.

863. **pone**, ' behind,' rare in Augustan Latin. Cf. Verg. A. 2. 725 *pone subit conjux*.

864. **eram**, sc. Phanium.

865. **Sophrona**. Cf. 830 note.

867. **suspenso gradu**, ' on tip-toe.'

869. **captans**, 'trying to catch.' Cf. Ov. Met. 10. 41–2 *Flebant exsangues animae:... nec Tantalus undam Captavit refugam*.

871. **mirificissumum**. In Augustan Latin adjectives in -*ficus*, -*dicus*, -*volus* are compared -*entior*, -*entissimus*.

873. **clanculum**, 'secretly:' a diminutive from *clam*. Note the unusual distance of *cum* from its noun *matre*.

874. **somnium**. Cf. 494.

utin haec ignoraret. Cf. 304 note.

877. **inaudivi**, 'I have chanced to hear.' This seems to be the regular sense of *inaudire*.

etiam dabo, 'I will tell you something more.' For this colloquial use of *dare* see Heaut. 10, Verg. E. 1. 18, Ov. Fast. 6. 434, Cic. Acad. 1. 3. 10: cf. *reddere* 320 perhaps, Hor. Sat. 2. 8. 80, Verg. A. 2. 323.

880. **adhibendae**. Cf. 827.

882. **quin ergo**. Cf. 209, 685 notes.

fecero, 'no sooner said than done.' Cf. 516.

883. **bene factum gaudeo**, 'I am delighted that all has gone well.'

Act IV. Scene 7. [V. 7.]

In the short soliloquy which closes the Act, Phormio prepares the audience for a new development of the plot. Armed with Geta's information, he sees his way to secure Phaedria from all trouble of returning the thirty minae, and himself from fulfilling the compact whereby the money was obtained.

884. **datam**, sc. *esse*. Cf. 153 note.

885–6. **eludendi ... adimere**. Note the change of construction. For *adimere* after *occasio* cf. Andr. 56 *studium alere*.

888–9. 'For this same money will have been given to Phaedria as grudgingly as it was given (to me).' Phormio says, the old men will be no better pleased when they learn the real destination of the money; but he can force their hand, and compel them to let Phaedria keep it.

NOTES. LINES 859-908.

hoc qui cogam, re ipsa repperi, 'I have discovered means to screw this out of them from the course events have taken.' *cogere* can take a double Acc. of the person forced, and of the thing extorted : cf. Ad. 490.

891. angiportum hoc proxumum, 'this alley hard by.' Both *angiportus*, mas. of the fourth decl. and *angiportum*, neut. of the second decl. were in use. The term was applied to those passages leading off the streets through a doorway, common in most old towns. Sometimes such a passage was a thoroughfare, sometimes a 'cul de sac.'

893. non eo. Cf. 447 note.

ACT V. SCENE 1 [8].

On the reappearance of Chremes and Demipho from their interview with Phanium, Phormio puts his new scheme into execution. He comes to fulfil his engagement like a 'man of honour.' Demipho makes very lame excuses to annul the compact and demand back the thirty minae. The parasite affects righteous indignation. He has already paid away the money, and broken off his betrothal in order to marry Phanium. If now this is not to be, the dowry at least must remain with him as satisfaction for the false position in which their indecision has placed him. Demipho waxes very angry and threatens summary justice; whereupon Phormio discloses his knowledge of the Lemnian intrigue. Chremes is utterly crushed. His brother urges him to make a clean breast of the affair to Nausistrata, and promises his mediation. Stung almost to frenzy by Phormio's taunts, Demipho tries to drag him off to the law-court. The parasite on his side attempts to get to the door of Chremes' house. There ensues a violent struggle, ended by the appearance of Nausistrata, who has heard the stentorian shouts of Phormio.

894. gratias habeo atque ago. The regular usage was to say *gratiam habeo*, but *gratias ago*.

896. This line is found in the MSS. after 905, where it is almost certainly misplaced by a copyist's error.

oppido. Cf. 317.

897. quantum potest. Cf. 674.

898. dilapidat, 'pitches away,' sc. like stones, 'makes ducks and drakes of it:' not found elsewhere in any classical writer.

903. recepissem, 'I had undertaken.'

semel, 'once' = 'at some former time,' thus used by Augustan authors, especially after *si*, *cum*, etc.

905. ut mi esset fides, 'to preserve my honour.'

906. idque adeo. Cf. 389.

908. ita uti par fuit, 'as was fitting.'

912. **potuit**, sc. *dari*.

913. **eam nunc extrudi**, so A, four later MSS. reading *nunc viduam extrudi*.

915. **inluditis me**. Terence constructs *inludere* thrice with the direct Acc., once with *in* and Acc., Eun. 942, once with *in* and Abl., And. 758. Cicero uses both the direct Acc., *in* with Acc., and also the Dat., which last construction is found also in Vergil and Tacitus. Its meaning is 'to make game of' or 'to spoil wantonly;' the sense 'to sport with,' given in L. and S. Dict. for *illudo chartis*, Hor. Sat. 1. 4. 139 is doubtful.

917. **contempserim**, lit. 'seeing that I have jilted her.'

918. **amittere**. Cf. 141 note.

922. **rescribi**, 'to be re-transferred.' Both at Athens and Rome the business of banking and money-changing was carried on in the marketplace by men called in Greek τραπεζῖται, in Latin *argentarii*.

923. **quodne ego discripsi porro** ... 'what? the money which I paid away again?' Note that the question is asked by *ne*, not by *quod*, which is not here interrogative. Cp. Pl. Tr. 358. Sometimes *-ne* is appended to an interrogative pronoun, when it emphasises the question, e.g. Hor. Sat. 2. 2. 107, ib. 2. 3. 295. Some critics consider this *-ne* as an affirmative particle, see Palmer on Pl. Am. 697.

925. **sin est ut velis**, periphrastic for *sin velis;* compare the use of *fore ut*.

928. **alterae**, archaic for *alteri*. Pronouns forming the Gen. and Dat. in *-ius* and *-i* are occasionally declined by Terence like a regular adjective in *-us -a -um*, e.g. Andr. 608 *nulli=nullius*, Eun. 1004 *mihi solae*. *Nulli consili* is also read Cic. Rosc. Com. 16, § 48.

929. **dabat**, 'was offering,' Gr. ἐδίδου.

930. **i hinc in malam rem** = *i in malam crucem*, 368 note. For scansion cf. 259 note, but the reading here is doubtful.

magnificentia, 'rodomontade.'

931. **fugitive**, 'vagabond,' lit. 'runaway slave.' Gr. δραπέτης.

932. **adeo** goes with *ignorarier*. 'Do you suppose that even now we know so little of you and your proceedings?'

933. **ut filius** etc. epexegetical of *hoc* etc.

937. **si porro esse odiosi pergitis**, 'if you continue to be troublesome.' For *porro*, here and 923, cf. 746 note.

940. **dotatis**, a hit at Chremes, whose wife was well *dotata*.

quid id nostra, sc. *refert?* Cf. 800.

942. **nullus sum**. Cf. 179.

943. **educat**. Terence more often uses *educere* in this sense.

sepultus sum, 'I'm dead and buried.' Cf. 1026.

944. **haec adeo**, 'these very things.' Cf. 389 note.
   illi. Phormio intentionally leaves the person unnamed. Of course he means Nausistrata.
   945. **eras.** Cf. 858.
   946. **missum te facimus**, 'we dismiss you.' Cf. 394 5 note.
   quid vis tibi? Cf. 843.
   947. **condonamus te.** Cf. 151 note. The Augustan construction is the Dative of the person.
   948. **malum!** 'the plague!' Cf. 723 note.
   ergo. Cf. 685 note.
   949. **puerili sententia**, 'your childish decisions:' *sententia* is here used in its proper sense as an 'expression of a determination.' Fleckeisen's conjecture *inconstantia* is quite gratuitous, as that meaning is given by *puerili*.
   950. **vŏlŏ : vŏlŏ.** Cf. 123 note.
   953. **nisi . . . scio**, 'I only know.' Cf. 475 note, Andr. 664.
   954. **monstri . . . simile**, 'it is like a judgment.' Cf. 705.
   inieci scrupulum, lit. 'a small pointed stone,' hence 'doubt,' 'anxiety,' 'difficulty.' Cf. 1019, Andr. 228, etc. A neuter form *scrupulum* or *scripulum* is used as the smallest division of weight, $\frac{1}{24}$ of an ounce. Tr. 'I have made them uneasy.'
   955. **hicine ut . . . auferat.** Cf. 304 note.
   957. **praesens**, 'resolute,' a classical usage. Compare the English phrase 'presence of mind.'
   959. The order is *neque iam te posse celare id uxorem tuam;* as usual *celare* takes a double Accusative.
   961. **placabilius est**, 'it is the better way to appease her.' Cf. 226 note.
   962. **nostro modo**, 'as we please.'
   963. Note the Hiatus at the change of speakers, cf. 146.
   attat. Cf. 600 note.
   haereo. For the tense cf. 447 note: cf. 780.
   964. **hi gladiatorio animo . . . viam**, 'they are planning an onset upon me in the spirit of desperadoes.' The metaphor in *gladiatorio* is of Roman origin. Terence very rarely makes an allusion so distinctly national. Cf. p. 16. The combats of gladiators were proverbially ferocious.
   966. **vos**, i.e. Chremes and his wife.
   967. **quom**, causal with Indic., cf. 23 note.
   e medio excessit, 'has departed this life.' Cf. 16, 1019 notes.
   suscepta est. Cf. 647 note.
   969. **ex re istius**, 'to your brother's advantage.' Cf. 526 note, Hor. Sat. 2. 6. 78.

istius may be dissyllabic of Synizesis, or the last syllable may be shortened.

970. **ain tu?** 'what do you mean, Sir?' A formula often used to express surprise, reproof, etc. **peregre.** Cf. 243 note.

971. **neque sis veritus,** 'and have had no respect for:' *vereor* in this sense with a Gen. is rare, but is once found in Cicero's letters.

972. **novo,** 'unheard of;' as often. **ēi.** Cf. 1030.

973. **lautum, Supine,** 'to wash away.'

974. **incensam dabo.** Cf. 559 note. For *dabo* cf. 877, 1027.

975. **ut ne.** Cf. 168 note.

lacrumis si extillaveris, 'even if you melt away in tears.'

976. **malum!** Cf. 723. Note *malum* used interjectionally, yet acting as antecedent to *quod*. **duint.** Cf. 123 note. The line is identical with Pl. Most. 655.

977. **adfectum esse.** Cf. 153 note.

978. **asportarier,** so used 551. Under the Empire *deportare* became a technical term implying transportation for life, usually to a small island, with loss of citizenship: while *relegare* was to banish beyond a certain distance from Rome for a stated period and with no *deminutio capitis*. Tr. 'to think that such a rascal is not sent a voyage at the public expense.'

981. **huc,** sc. *eamus*.

983. **enim nequeo,** 'I really can't.' Cf. 113 note.

iniuria, 'action for assault.' Cf. 329.

984. **ergo.** Cf. 685 note.

985. **rape hunc,** 'drag him away.'

sic agitis? 'is that your plan?'

987. **valet.** Cf. 358 note.

non taces? 'won't you hold your tongue?' Cf. 447 note.

989. **est ubi,** Gr. ἔστιν ὅτε, 'sometime.'

ACT V. SCENE 2 [9].

With insolent triumph Phormio discloses to the outraged wife her husband's infamy. Demipho tries to intercede for his wretched brother, at first with small success. Phormio improves the occasion. He wins from Nausistrata a practical assurance that Phaedria shall be allowed to keep his bride, that the money paid shall not be asked for, and last, but not least, an invitation for himself to supper, to which they all go in as the curtain falls[1].

---

[1] In Roman theatres the curtain was lowered (*aulaea premere*) to the floor, or perhaps drawn under the stage at the commencement of an

NOTES. LINES 970–1021.   169

990. **qui nominat me—?** Nausistrata begins to speak while she is scarcely out of the door. Before she has time to finish her sentence (with *homo* perhaps), her eyes fall on the termination of the violent struggle before the house, and she breaks off with an exclamation of surprise. This explains *qui*, which otherwise would have been *quis*. Cf. 618 note.

991. **quis hic homo est?** 'who is this fellow here?' Cf. 618 note.

992. **hicine ut ... respondeat.** Cf. 304 note.

993. **creduas.** All MSS. give *credas;* but the archaic form seems necessary for the metre. Plautus uses *creduam, creduas, creduat:* also *creduis, creduit.*

994. **abi.** Cf. 59 note.

totus friget, 'all as cold as a stone,' i.e. with fright. Cf. Pl. Most. 4. 2. 1 *totus gaudeo.*

998. **quod.** Cf. 155 note.

1001. **tibi narret?** 'is he to tell the tale for you?'

factum est abs te sedulo, 'you have managed matters nicely.'

1005. **mi homo!** 'my good man!'

1009. **hodie,** 'in our time.'

1012. **haecine.** Cf. 58 note.

1014. The order is *non nego eum meritum esse culpam in hac re.*

1015. **sed ea quin sit ignoscenda?** 'but why should that be unpardonable?' **quin** = 'why not,' cf. 209. Donatus, followed by Bentley, considered the phrase as an Aposiopesis, *negare non poteris* or the like being understood. Others repeat *non nego* before *quin*, sc. *sed non nego quin ea sit ignoscenda*, which does not seem very forcible.

verba fiunt mortuo: a doubtful phrase, (1) 'you are wasting words on the dead;' or, 'you might as well talk to the dead,' sc. as to Nausistrata: cf. Pl. Bacch. 519 *nihilo plus referet Quam si ad sepulchrum mortuo dixit logos.*

(2) 'his funeral oration is being pronounced,' a sarcastic allusion to Demipho's feeble excuses for Chremes, which are represented as the *laudatio* usually delivered at a funeral, perhaps here suggested by *sepultus sum* 943, cf. 1026.

1016. **tua ... tuo,** objective use.

1019. **e medio abiit,** 'has departed.' Cf. 16, 967 notes.

qui, attracted into the gender of *scrupulus.*

scrupulus. Cf. 954 note.

1021. **quid ego aequo animo,** sc. *feram?* 'how can I bear it calmly?'

Act, and raised again at the conclusion (*aulaea tollere*). Cf. Hor. Ep. 2. 1. 189 *quattuor aut plures aulaea premuntur in horas,* Verg. G. 3. 2 *purpurea intexti tollant aulaea Britanni.*

cupio ... defungier, 'I wish, wretched woman that I am, that this were now the end.'

defungier probably impersonal, as in Ad. 507 *utinam hic sit modo defunctum*. The translation, 'I should like to die at once in my misery,' seems to agree neither with the following words nor with Ad. 507.

1022. **quid sperem?** 'what can I hope for?' Fleckeisen's conjecture, *qui id sperem*, 'how can I hope for it,' is very plausible.

1024. **magis expetenda,** 'more attractive.'

1026. **exequias Chremeti ... ire,** a formula used in giving notice of a funeral. Note the omission of the preposition before *exequias*.

1027. **sic dabo,** 'that's my style,' or 'such shall be my revenge.' *dare = facere* is common in colloquial Latin, in Lucretius and Vergil, less frequent in Cicero and Livy. We find such phrases as *dare finem, cuneum, motus, ruinas, discessum, impetum*, etc. = *facere finem*, etc. Munro on Lucr. 4. 41 quotes Max Müller, Science of Language, 2nd series, p. 224, 'in Latin it was equally impossible to distinguish between the roots *dâ* and *dhâ*, because the Romans had no aspirated dentals; but such was the good sense of the Romans that, when they felt they could not efficiently keep the two roots apart, they kept only one, *dare*, to give, and replaced the other *dare*, to place or to make, by different verbs, such as *ponere, facere*.'

It seems possible that such uses of *dare* as are given above may be survivals in popular or poetical language of *dare* from root *dhâ*. Cf. 974, etc.

1028. **faxo.** Cf. 308 note. Two MSS. read *faxo tali sit mactatus*.

mactatum, 'victimised.' For the various senses of *mactare* see Lewis and Short. With this reading note *hīc*; cf. 266 note.

1030. **habet ... ogganniat,** 'she has something to din (lit. snarl) into his ears as long as he lives.' Note *ei*.

1031. **at meo merito,** sc. *hoc videtur factum.* Cf. 1033. At first sight it looks as if this repetition of the same phrase (1031 and 1033) were due to some corruption of the text: but in the mouth of the outraged Nausistrata it is perhaps natural enough.

1033. **minume gentium!** 'not the least in the world!' *gentium* is a partitive Genitive, cf. *nusquam gentium*, ποῦ γῆς, etc.

1034. **fieri infectum non potest,** 'cannot be made unmade;' this *infectum* is a compound of *in* and *factum*, to be distinguished from *infectus*, Perf. Part. Pass. of *inficio*, 'I stain,' 'corrupt.'

1035. **purgat,** 'he apologises.'

1037. **Nausistratā** like Sophronā, Phaedriā. cf. 830 note.

prius quam is thus used with a Pres. Indic. when the event or act referred to is regarded as certain, otherwise with a Subj., e. g. Ad. 583 *prius quam ad portam venias*.

1047. **discedo**, 'I get off,' colloquial. Cf. 773. The persons among whom lines 1046-7 are apportioned seem to have been confused in the MSS. A omits *satis*.

1048. **mihin** is monosyllabic.

1049. **summus**, sc. *amicus*, 'most devoted to.'

1050. **at** emphasises the affirmation.

quod potero, 'as far as I possibly can.'

ecastor, according to Gellius, was used exclusively by women, *hercle* by men. Either sex employed *pol*. Cf. 735 note.

1052. **quod** here and in 1053 is a Cognate Acc. Cf. 259.

1053. **me ad cenam voca**. By a professional parasite this would doubtless be interpreted as a standing invitation.

1055. **iudex noster**. Cf. 1045.

faxo aderit. Cf. 308 note.

Cantor. A Roman Comedy was divided into spoken dialogue in Iambic Senarii *diverbia* and the passages in any other metre which were delivered to a musical accompaniment *'cantica'*. The term *Canticum* was also used in a more restricted sense to denote a lyrical monologue, of which Plautus has numerous examples. Terence only three, and those very short, Andr. 481-5, ib. 625-638, Ad. 610-6.

We learn from Livy 7. 2 that, in order to save his voice, Livius Andronicus placed a boy on the stage to sing the words of *cantica*, while Livius himself acted the part in dumb show. This practice was adopted by others, and it seems from Hor. A. P. 155 *donec Cantor 'vos plaudite' dicat* that the usual request for applause was uttered by this singer, who is to be distinguished from the accompanist *Tibicen*.

It is, however, possible that '*Cantor*' in Hor. A. P. merely means 'actor,' as Cicero pro Sest. 55. 118 uses *cantores* as equivalent to *histriones*.

In all Terence's plays the MSS. mark the speaker of *plaudite* by ω. Bentley thought this to be a corruption of CA. (for *Cantor*, but, as the actors are often indicated by letters of the Greek alphabet in the order of their appearance, it is more probable that ω was appropriated to the speaker of the last words.

INDEX TO NOTES.

(*References are to the number of the lines. Words distinguished by an asterisk are ἅπαξ λεγόμενα. When the same word has been noted more than once, but in different case, person, tense, etc., the references will be found under the form which occurs first; and when the same point recurs several times, references are given in the place where it is first noted.*)

A.
a fratre, 732.
ab animo, 340.
abduc, 410.
abi, 59.
Ablative (after esse, facere, fieri), 137.
abs,   } 188.
absque. }
Accusative and Infinitive (in excited speech), 153.
Accusative (without a verb), 480.
— (*adverbial*), 155.
— (*cognate*), 259.
actum ne agas, 419.
actutum, 852.
ad (*after its case*), 524.
ad ditem dari, 653.
ad restim res redit, 686.
adduc, 309.
adeo, 389.
adsient, 313.
adventi, 154.
advorsum (*after its case*), 427.
advorsum stimulum calces, 78.
Aedilibus Curulibus, note on Didascalia.
Affirmative phrases, 315.
aibat, 480.
ain tu, 970.
aliquot hos sumam dies, 831-2.
Alliteration, 1.
alternae (= alteri*, 928.
Ambivius Turpio, note on Didascalia.
amitte, 141.
ampliatio, 457.

Analytic phrases, 394-5.
angiportum, 891.
animam debet, 661.
antehac, 4.
antiquom, 67.
Apollodorus, note on Didascalia.
Aposiopesis, 51.
appellassis, 742.
apud me, 204.
argentum est ultro obiectum, 760.
artem musicam, 17
asportarier, 978.
Assonance, 18.
asymbolum, 339.
Asyndeton, 556.
atavo, 395.
attat, 600.
au, 754.
audisset bene, 20.
auribus teneo lupum, 506.
autem, 502-3.

B.
belua, 601.
-bilis (*adjectives in*), 226.
bona venia, 378.

C.
cantilenam eandem canis, 495.
Cantor, 1055.
carcer, 373.
-ce, 442.
cědŏ, 197.
cessavit, 475.
Chremem (*declension of*), 63.
circumiri, 613.
clanculum, 87ɔ.
commodum, 614.

commutabitis verba, 638.
compluria, 611.
concrepuit ostium, 840.
condicionem, 578.
condonamus te, 947.
confutavit, 477.
conicito, 166.
consuetudinem, 161.
consuleres, 468.
*contortor, 374.
contra, 521.
*convasassem, 190.
conveniat (*with Acc.*), 719.
cordi est, 800.
cotidiana, 160.
credo (*parenthetical*), 40.
creduas, 993.

D.

da locum melioribus, 522.
dare = facere, 1027.
dare se dixit, 532.
date operam, 30.
de ('*in accordance with*'), 481.
de integro, 174.
defetiscar, 589.
defungier, 1021.
delibutum gaudio, 856.
demenso, 43.
depecisci morte, 166.
deputare in lucro, 246.
derivem, 323.
di nos respiciunt, 817.
dicam, 127.
dici nos bonos studemus, 767.
dictio, 293.
*dilapidat, 898.
discedi possiet, 773.
dudum, 289.
-dum (*enclitic*), 329.
duplici spe utier, 603.

E.

e medio excessit, 967.
ecastor, 1050.
eccere, 319.
eccum, 464.
edepol, 735.

effutiretis, 746.
Ellipse (of sit), 46.
— (*of Infinitive clause*), 113.
— (*of principal verb*), 38.
em, 52.
emunxi argento senes, 682.
enicas, 384.
enim, 113.
enimvero, 555.
Epidicazomenos, note on Didascalia.
equidem, 539.
ergo, 685.
erilem filium, 39.
esses proferens, 394-5.
etiam (*intensive*), 474, 542.
eu (εὖ), 398.
ex re, 969.
excutiam me, 586.
exequias Chremeti, 1026.
exorarier, 535-6.

F.

face, 397.
facessat, 635.
factum volo, 787.
faeneratum, 493.
familia, 570-1.
faxo, 308.
ferietur, 47.
fidem, 469.
foris, 308.
Fors Fortuna, 841.
fugitans litium, 623.
fugitive, 931.
functus (*construction of*), 281.
Future Imperative (*for Pres. Imper.*), 143.
Future Perfect (*expressing certainty*), 516.

G.

gallina cecinit, 708.
garri modo, 496.
Genitive (*in* -u = Gr. ου), note on Didascalia.
Genitive (in -i *for* -us), 154.
Genitive (*after participles*), 623.
genium, 44.

Gerund (in -undi), 22.
gladiatorio animo, 964.
gratias habeo atque ago, 894.
grex, 32.
gynaeceum, 862.

H.
hariolare, 492.
hariolus, } 708-9.
haruspex,
hem, 52.
Hiatus, Introduction. p. 31.
hic (*quantity of*), 266.
hic viciniae, 95.
hisce, 442.
hoc age, 435.
hoc qui cogam re ipsa repperi, 888-9.
horunc, 290.

I.
i in malam crucem, 368.
-ibam (*for* -iebam), 480.
ii, 41.
ilicet, 208.
ilico, 88, 195.
illi = illic, 91.
Imperfect colloquial use of, 858.
Imperfect Subj. (*for Pluperf.*), 108.
in diem abiit, 781.
in eodem luto haesitas, 780.
in malo quaerere crucem, 543-4.
in manum dari, 633 4.
in medio, 16.
inaudivi, 877.
incensam dabo, 974.
Indicative in dependent sentences, 358.
ineptis, 420.
infectum, 1034.
Infinitive (*in* -ier), 92.
— (*Historic*), 92, 117.
ingenium, 70.
inieci scrupulum, 954.
initiabunt, 49.
iniuriarum dicam, 329.
inluditis me, 915.
inpendent (*with Acc.*), 180.
inpingam, 439.
inpluvium, 707.

insistam, 192.
intristi, 318.
inventas reddam, 559.
ipsus, 178.
istuc, 58.
ita fugias ne praeter casam, 768.
ita . . . ut (*in asseverations*), 807.
ita uti par fuit, 908.

L.
lacrumis si extillaveris, 975.
laterem lavem, 186.
lectum est, 53.
liberalis, 623.
lites paratae, 133.
logi, 493.
Ludis Romanis, note on Didascalia.

M.
mactatum infortunio, 1028.
magistratus adi, 403.
magnificentia, 930.
male factum, 751.
malis exemplis, 688.
malum (*interjectional*), 723.
mederi (*with Acc.?*), 822.
memini, 74.
-met, 172.
minas, 410.
minume gentium, 1033.
mirabar si quicquam, 490.
mirarier, 92.
mirificissumum, 871.
miseritum est, 501.
modo ut, 59.
monstra, 705, 954.

N.
nam quod = quodnam, 200.
narras, 401.
natalis dies, 48.
ne (*with Pres. Imper.*), 664.
ne quid verborum duit, 713.
nervom, 325.
nescio quod, 193.
nil = non, 142.
nimium quantum libuit, 643.
nisi (= *but*), 475.

INDEX. 175

non = nonne, 119.
nostin, 64.
nullus es. 179.
num quid vis, 151.
numquam tu odio tuo me vinces, 849.

O.

O, Introduction, p. 31.
ob rem, 526.
obstupefecit, 284.
obtundes, 515.
ogganniat, 1030.
oppido (*adverb*), 317.
oppositus est pignori, 661.
opus *constructions of*, 440, 563.
oratione, 5.

P.

paedagogus, 144.
palaestra, 484.
pallio, 844.
parasitus, 28.
paulo, 822.
per- (*prefix*), 558.
per silentium, 30.
perdidi, 386.
perdite, 82.
perduint, 123.
peregre, 243.
pergit hercle, 849.
perperam, 745.
phaleratis dictis, 500.
Phormio, 27.
pistrinum, 249.
placabilius, 961.
platea, 215.
Pleonastic phrases, 80, 89.
Pluperfect force of), 594, 651.
pluscula, 665.
poeta vetus, 1.
pone ('*behind*', 863.
popularis, 35.
portitores, 150.
postilla, 347.
postquam, 1.
poteretur. 469.
potest (*impersonal*), 303.
potis est, 379.
praesens ('*resolute*'), 957.

praesto, 51.
precatorem, 140.
preci, 547.
Present Indicative for Pres. Subj.), 447, 737.
— *to express intention*'), 486, 532.
Present Infinitive (*for Future*, 532.
priusquam *construction of*, 1037.
pro *interjection*, 351.
protelet, 213.
protinam. 190.
Proverbial phrases, 78, 186, 203, 318, 419, 506, 768, 780.
provinciam, 72.
-pte, 172.
pudet, 392.
puerili sententia, 949.
punctum temporis, 184.

Q.

quantum est qui vivont, 853.
quantum potest, 674.
qui *causal*, 156.
qui *concessive*, 153.
qui *Abl.*, 123.
qui *ana* quis *in questions*, 618,990.
quid, 64.
quid agitur, 610.
quid ais, 199.
quid haec videntur, 792.
quid ni, 64.
quid tu, 798.
quidnam hic sibi volt, 843.
quin, 209.
quod 155.
quod es dignus, 519.
quodne ego discripsi, 923.
quom (*spelling of*, 9.
quom *causal or concessive with Indic.*, 23.
quom maxume, 204.

R.

ratione, 297.
-re *termination of 2nd pers. sing. pass.*, 173.
redducere, 86.
redit, 55.

refert (*construction of*), 723.
regem, 70.
regnas, 405.
reicere, 18.
relicuom, 37.
rellatum, 21.
repudium renuntiet, 677.
rescribi, 922.
restitui in integrum, 451.
ringitur, 341.
rufus, 51.

S.
*saevidicis, 213.
sane, 667.
satin id est, 683.
Scansion (*peculiarities of*), 9, 14, 123, 176, 259, 284, 307, 315, 370, 411, 535, 706, 707, 969, 1030, Introduction, pp. 27–31.
scapulas perdidi, 76.
scibit, 765.
scita, 110, 820.
scriptura, 5.
serva, 212.
servom hominem, 292.
sepultus sum, 943.
Sequence of Tenses, 381, 592.
sescentas, 668.
si (*expressing a wish*), 535.
sic erit, 801.
siet, 313.
sis (= si vis), 59.
sodes, 103.
somnia, 494.
stares cum illo, 267.
statim, 790.
suat, 491.
subcenturiatus, 230.
Subject omitted before Infin., 233.
Subjunctive (*Imperf. for Pluperf.*), 108.
—— (*in questions*), 122.
subolet, 474.
sudabis satis, 628.
Sunium, 837.
Superlatives in -umus, 125.

suscepisse, 647.
suspenso gradu, 867.
Syncopated Forms, 13, 198.
Synizesis, 18, 201, 299, Introduction, pp. 30–31.

T.
talentum, 393, 644.
tandem ('*after all*'), 231, 701.
-te, 172.
tenes, 214.
tibiis inparibus, note on Didascalia.
tonstrina, 89.
tradunt operas mutuas, 267.
tristis, 57.
tu te idem melius feceris, 426.
tum (*particle of transition*), 549.

V.
ultro, 360.
unciatim, 43.
usque ad, 327.
usus venit, 73.
ut (*causal*), 774.
ut (*introducing a wish*), 687.
ut ne, 168.
utibile, 690.

V (CONSONANTAL).
vanitatis, 526.
vapula, 850.
vel, 143.
venit in mentem, 154.
verba fiunt mortuo, 1015.
Verbal Substantives, 293.
verbero, 684.
vereor (*with Gen.*), 971.
verum enim, 555.
videas te atque illum, ut narras, 368.
videre (*construction of*), 7, 621-2.
vincibilem, 226.
vis boni, 107.
volo (*construction of*), 102, 151, 787.
volup, 610.
vorsuram solves, 780.

THE END.

www.ingramcontent.com/pod-product-compliance
Lightning Source LLC
Chambersburg PA
CBHW022112160426
43197CB00009B/987